AKITAS
KW-107

Front endpapers: *The proud and dignified Akita has been designated as a national monument of Japan, his native country.* **(left)** *Owner, John D'Alessio.* **(right)** *Owners, Joel and Jeanette Ward.*

Title page: *The Akita is a very people-oriented dog that thrives on human companionship. Owner, Edward J. Finnegan, Jr.*

Photo credits: *Isabelle Francais and Ron Reagan.*

Drawings by *Scott Boldt, Richard Crammer, Richard Davis, Andrew Prendimano, John Quinn, and Alexandra Suchenka.*

The text of this book is the result of the joint efforts of the author and the editorial staff of T.F.H. Publications, Inc., which is the originator of all sections of the book except the chapters dealing with the history of the Akita and the breed description. Additionally, the portrayal of canine pet products in this book is for general instructive value only; the appearance of such products does not necessarily constitute an endorsement by the author, the publisher, or the owners of the dogs portrayed in this book.

t.f.h.

© Copyright 1994 by T.F.H. Publications, Inc.

Distributed in the UNITED STATES to the Pet Trade by T.F.H. Publications, Inc., One T.F.H. Plaza, Neptune City, NJ 07753; distributed in the UNITED STATES to the Bookstore and Library Trade by National Book Network, Inc. 4720 Boston Way, Lanham MD 20706; in CANADA to the Pet Trade by H & L Pet Supplies Inc., 27 Kingston Crescent, Kitchener, Ontario N2B 2T6; Rolf C. Hagen Ltd., 3225 Sartelon Street, Montreal 382 Quebec; in CANADA to the Book Trade by Macmillan of Canada (A Division of Canada Publishing Corporation), 164 Commander Boulevard, Agincourt, Ontario M1S 3C7; in the United Kingdom by T.F.H. Publications, PO Box 15, Waterloov-ille PO7 6BQ; in AUSTRALIA AND THE SOUTH PACIFIC by T.F.H. (Australia), Pty. Ltd., Box 149, Brookvale 2100 N.S.W., Australia; in NEW ZEALAND by Brooklands Aquarium Ltd. 5 McGiven Drive, New Plymouth, RD1 New Zealand; in Japan by T.F.H. Publications, Japan—Jiro Tsuda, 10-12-3 Ohjidai, Sakura, Chiba 285, Japan; in SOUTH AFRICA by Multipet Pty. Ltd., P.O. Box 35347, Northway, 4065, South Africa. Published by T.F.H. Publications, Inc.
Manufactured in the United States of America by T.F.H. Publications, Inc.

AKITAS

EDITA VAN DER LYN

Alert, affectionate, and handsome, the Akita has been a highly prized family dog and protector for thousands of years. Owner, Gayle Pierce.

Contents

Dedication

This book is dedicated to the memory of my first Akita, *Akita Tani's Aka Kosho.* *"Sans Peur et Sans Reproche."*

Acknowledgments

Arigato: To Don and Twyla Lusk, of the Arashi Hoshi Akitas, whose generously given assistance in verifying facts and information based on their visits to Japan has been invaluable in compiling this book. It is their special kind of integrity, both in their breeding procedures and 'standing by' to help any Akita owner/fancier, that will keep this truly remarkable breed poised at the pinnacle of perfection as far as is humanly possible.

A very special mention is due Liz Harrell of the Akita Tani Kennels, whose continued and knowledgable work in the inexhaustible field of genetics plays a major role in the guidance of both neophyte and established Akita breeders. The ethical breeding practices of Miss Harrell, a pioneer of the breed from its very beginnings in this country, were and continue to be an inspiration to those truly interested in furthering this noble breed on its highest possible level of development. Indeed, the Akita Fancy owes eternal thanks to this First Lady of the Akita.

Unsurpassed by any other breed in dignity and steadfastness, the Akita also enjoys clowning about for the amusement of his family and himself.

Facing page: *The sparkle in the eyes of an Akita puppy is surely a convincing indication that he is a most loyal and trustworthy friend. Owner, Edward J. Finnegan, Jr.*

The Akita Mystique

The apex of Nippon imports in the world of canines is the Akita-Inu (Akita Dog), a creature as Japanese as Haiku poetry and tea ceremonies, the Kabuki Theater and Bonsai cultivation. An irresistible attention-getter, the Akita personifies all the enigmatic character of the Orient. Your first impression is that of an immensely powerful and imposing animal with a massive chest and a head suggestive of a bear. It is possessed of a dignity of expression that defies description.

One of the most outstanding physical characteristics is the uniquely positioned ears—rather small, erect and triangular, set somewhat to the side of the head and slanting forward. Another is its bushy tail, carried over the back. Formidable in size, majestic in appearance, the Akita creates the impression of instant grandeur, commanding immediate respect. Combine this physical stature with a sober, calm disposition, fearless yet steady, and you have a dog that is not given to tantrums; one that does not go berserk when confronted with unusual or sudden stressful situations. Even as a puppy, the Akita displays a dignity virtually unknown in puppies of most other breeds. He goes through a sort of prestigious kindergarten stage, equipped with built-in self-control. Even the battle of the puddle and the tug-of-war which inevitably succeed a pup's

first time on a collar and lead are matters to be taken in stride.

With an uncanny ability, the Akita adjusts to and accepts widely varying circumstances and lifestyles; not as an imposition upon his canine freedom but as a way of life. Yet at the same time, he retains a remarkably aloof and free spirit. In short, disciplined social behavior, quiet dignity and the cat-like grace with which he moves make this beautiful dog a highly desirable living companion. He is an ever-patient playmate for small fry, a no-nonsense protector of family and home. Most of all, he is a joy to own at all times and in any given situation. Is it any wonder the Japanese refer to the Akita as their *Ichiban Number One*? And speak of him affectionately as being tender in heart and strong in strength—the dog that begins where others leave off.

HISTORY

Flamboyant with romanticism, a mixture of fact and fiction, of fantasy and controversy, the Akita's history embraces far more material than space for coverage permits. Historians are a special breed of scholar as they delve into the past, sifting through contradictions and generalities. Notwithstanding the authenticity of official records, not all sources are infallible.

As a pure breed, the Akita dates

Although the Akita has enjoyed a prominent history of hunting and working outdoors, he is perfectly comfortable within the protective confines of your four walls.

back over thirty centuries and is the largest of the seven Japanese purebred breeds which were declared a National Monument by the Japanese Ministry of Education. Classified by size, the five medium dogs were: Hokkaido-Inu, Koshi-no-Inu, Kai-Inu, Kishu-Inu and Shikoku-Inu. The Shiba is the small Japanese dog and the Akita, the only large one.

Apart from having been declared a National Monument by the Japanese Ministry of Education, the Akita has become a status symbol in other areas

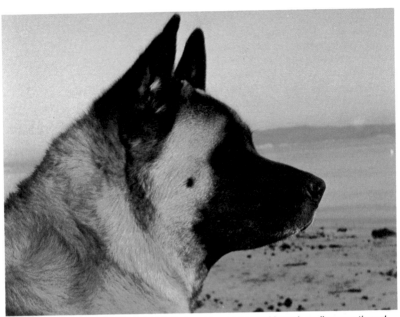

Head study of the Akita—the Akita's head is massive although well proportioned to his tremendous body.

bearing witness to the esteem in which the breed is held by the Japanese. Tachibana-Go was the model for a postage stamp, for instance. The hides of favorite Akitas are tanned and preserved in loving memory. If an owner no longer is able to care for his Akita champion, the Japanese government will subsidize maintainance for as long as is necessary.

Additionally, the Akita is considered a good luck charm and omen. When a new baby is born, or when there is sickness in a family, a small carved statue of an Akita is given. Working women know the Akita has no equal as a babysitter. Absolutely trustworthy, he patiently and tolerantly submits to ear-tugging and tail-pulling from small fries while shielding them from harm and protecting them, with his life if necessary, from any intruders, be it man or beast.

The Akita derives its name from Akita Prefecture, a region at the northern tip of Honshu Island in Japan whence the dog hails. This is a rocky, mountainous country with a severe climate. No doubt these territorial conditions are responsible for the breed's superior size and strength, massive build, and a power of endurance that will not quit.

The Akita was first known as Odate dog (Odate is a city—also called 'Dog City'—in Akita Prefecture and was the venue of the Headquarters Show May

1977) but the name was then changed to *Akita-Inu* (Inu meaning 'dog') prior to being the first of the seven purebred Japanese dogs to be declared a National Monument in July, 1931, in order to preserve this deserving breed. Due to a series of unfortunate circumstances, the Akita had suffered severe setbacks from time to time, bordering on extinction. Especially cruel to the survival of the Akita as a breed were the effects of World War II with extreme shortages of food and other commodities. Warm clothing was obtained from dog and cat fur. The Akita became a target to be hunted down, captured and killed. Many were clubbed to death and concerned owners were forced to place their beloved dogs with farmers living in remote mountain areas, making it appear as if they were being used as guard dogs.

Stepping further back into history, Japan had a fatal rabies outbreak in 1899 and by 1924, 3205 cases had been reported.

These puppies enjoy wrestling and rumbling on the lawn.

Many stray dogs, including Akitas, were destroyed.

During the seventeenth and eighteenth centuries, dog fighting as a sport and entertainment, especially in surrounding rural areas, farther jeopardized the Akita's survival as a pure breed. To produce a dog of superior size, that was both aggressive and powerful, the Akita was crossed with the Tosa fighting dog from Shikoku Island. Some areas had an ordinance to ban this cruel and gory sport, but in spite of this it was carried on in remote places after dark. However, in 1915 and 1916 dog fighting was again legally resumed and in full swing. Dogs were brought back from areas where dog fights had been banned and once more the Tosa was pitted against the Akita and both were liberally interbred. The result of this interbreeding was that the Akita's original inherent hunting instinct and gentle disposition were infused with the aggressive fighting traits of the Tosa. The cross was referred to as: Shin-Akita (the New Akita Dog).

The purebred Akita thus teetered on the brink of extinction until 1927, when Mr. Shigeie (Mokke) Izumi, then mayor of Odate, organized the Akita-Inu Hozonkai (Akiho) with the purpose of preserving the original Japanese Akita. It may be that this organization was farther advanced by a certain Professor Watase's survey of the Akita Dog as a proposed Natural Monument and finally led to the restoration of the breed. Had the good professor been less concerned or determined to save this remarkable Japanese breed, we might never have known this beautiful animal as we know him today.

Considering that the Akita is a hunter par excellence, it is fortunate that despite the crossbreedings with the Tosa, neither his hunting instincts, nor his naturally gentle disposition, could be entirely obliterated. The Matagi (hunter) people who are related by language to the practically extinct Ainu tribe of Hokkaido, hunt for bear, deer, and wild boar. Two Akitas, for instance a male and a female, will track down the vicious 800-pound Yezo bear, and hold him at bay until the hunters arrive. The Yezo has been known to attack villages. An interesting characteristic of the hunting Akita is that he hunts silently and even if provoked to fight, he will not give warning with a preparatory growl. The Akita has also proven himself a worthy

Facing page: This Akita pup is still growing. Some Akitas bear a striking resemblance to the German Shepherd Dog; however, the Akita's head, in general, is much larger and his tail curls over his back.

The Akita Mystique

hunting companion for smaller game and fowl and will retrieve with the same tender mouth associated with the more usual hunting dogs.

The Akita's resemblance (and it is just that, a resemblance) to some arctic breeds is explained in investigative writings from antiquarians who have traced the Akita's origin back to the arctic-type hunting dogs of Eurasian tribes several millenniums B.C. Hirokichi Saito, one of Japan's most eminent authorities on animal life, attests that skeletons of dogs unearthed and reconstructed some 6,000 years ago, as well as ancient clay images, bear some resemblance to the Akita. The skeletons were dug from burial mounds dating as far back as the New Stone Age. Less than four hundred years ago, however, before the Akita became

Akitas make reliable and responsible mothers; a hungry litter of newborns is enough to keep this patient bitch occupied for a ''dog's day''plus one!

a pure breed, there had been infusions of bloodlines from the large Chinese Chows and Northern-type dogs. Akitas have the bushy, curled tail and upstanding ear as do the Chow Chow, Malamute, Siberian Husky, Samoyed and Spitz-related breeds But this is where the resemblance ends and even the Akita's ears are of a shape and position like no other breed of dog.

INTRODUCTION TO THE UNITED STATES

There is a particularly romantic flavor to the Akita's introduction to American soil. Although there is factual truth about U.S. servicemen's having brought over Akitas after World War II, the breed's unique distinction is that the *very first* Akita to come to this country belonged to Helen Keller who although grievously handicapped, transformed her personal disaster of a sightless, speechless, soundless world into a triumph of human courage.

In 1937, while on an extensive lecturing tour of Japan, Helen Keller, already a legend and revered in that county, visited Akita City. Previously when in Tokyo, she had visited the statue of the famed Akita Hachiko at Shibuya Station. She had been deeply touched by the story of this dog's devotion and faithfulness. When Keller expressed a desire to

An unexpected and rather disarming visitor, this Akita stands on his hind legs waiting to be greeted.

own an Akita, wheels were set in motion to accomplish this. In April of that year, a litter of Akita puppies was born in Odate City and two of the males were destined to make Akita history.

Although Akitas, at that time,

The Akita Mystique

were still scarce, a Mr. Ichiro Ogasawara, employed in the police department, decided to part with a beautiful *goma*-colored puppy about three months old. When the lady left Akita City in June of that year, the puppy was ceremoniously presented to her as a gift of friendship from Japan. The puppy was named "Kamikaze" (Divine Wind) commemorating the flight of a monoplane of that name that made aviation history by flying from Tokyo to London in just fifty hours. A deep bond grew between the dog and his mistress who called him 'angel in fur.' When she lost him to distemper at barely eight months of age in spite of every precautionary measure she could take, her silent world was clouded with grief.

Finally Helen Keller wrote to Mr. Ogasawara, chief of police, who assuaged her sadness by making arrangements to have the litter brother of her beloved Kamikaze shipped to the United States. Again, the dog was a gift from the Japanese. Kenzan-Go at the age of two, and after what must have been a bewildering thirty-one days at sea, was welcomed by his overjoyed mistress on July 1, 1939. Despite later hostilities between the two countries, Helen Keller, the lady "*sans peur et sans reproche*," had created her own monument of courage. As Hemingway wrote: "courage is intangible, grace under pressure; a quality of mind that enables one to encounter difficulties with valor."

IN THE U.S. AND OTHER COUNTRIES

The most prominent of American-bred Akitas was Akita Tani's Shoyo-Go who left an indelible heritage of persistent quality, dominant in appearance as well as disposition, in his progeny. Shoyo, a 135 pound gorgeous red sesame with white markings and a black mask, was bred by Al and Liz Harrell of the Akita Tani Kennels. He appears in most of the pedigrees of today's top Akitas and was sired by the Japanese Grand Champion Kinsho-Go. Japanese Grand Champion Kongo-Go, perhaps the greatest of all Japanese Akitas of all time, was his grandsire.

Shoyo-Go himself was top male Akita in 1965 and 1966 and one of the top ten in 1967. He was also the first Akita to place at the Chicago International in 1967; best stud dog in 1965 and, at the end of a brilliant record as a sire, was best veteran in 1970. He died at the age of thirteen leaving a legacy still unequalled. Unquestionably Shoyo would have attained championship status had AKC recognition come earlier, but the breed was not recognized until 1973.

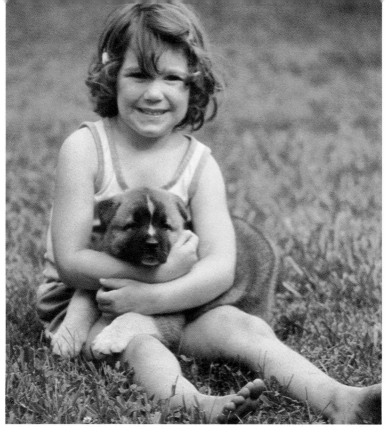

Akitas make wonderful companions for children—it is not uncommon for Japanese women to rely on their Akitas to babysit their children—in this capacity, the Akita has proven unsurpassable.

Akitas in Canada are a relatively recent event. The breed was recognized by the Canadian Kennel Club January 1, 1975, and in March, 1975, the first Akita gained Canadian championship. The goal of Canadian breeders is to protect and promote the breed; to prevent crossbreedings; and to provide factual information, knowledge and education to acquaint the Canadian public with this beautiful dog.

Akitas are steadily growing in popularity around the world and many breed experts have come forward to write about this fascinating Japanese treasure. *The Book of the Akita* (H-1075) published by T.F.H. has long been a *sine qua non* for all fanciers and is still available from the publisher. A relatively new breed in the United States, the Akita continues to turn heads and inspire new writings.

A Description of the Breed

The breed's dignified presence is its most distinctive quality. Each element described in the standard is designed to contribute to the overall distinctiveness. Emphasized is the head. The overall broad and triangular shape creates an harmonious whole with the triangular shape of ears and eyes, creating the Akita's alert and fearless expression. The tail is large and bushy and must curl over the dog's back. It should never trail behind or be carried erect.

In movement, the Akita combines power with precision and smoothness; a natural movement that is purposeful and expressive.

The Akita is reserved, silent and remains unruffled by minor irritations. When confronting other canines, he assumes the dominant role; he is alert and will not back down when challenged. Toward his owners, he is extremely affectionate, devoted and protective. He is friendly with people in general, but aloof. Trespassers, when confronted by this powerful dog, prefer to keep a respectful distance.

AS A COMPANION

Although the Akita has a firm hold as a top show dog, there are, comparatively, more potential owners interested in a compatible family pet and alert companion that is easy to live with. The breed's protective instincts are inherent. There is no need to jeopardize them by channelling them into any specific guard and/or attack-training avenues and, perhaps, end up with a canine 'loaded gun,' as has been the case with some dogs of other breeds. The danger is very real since the average owner is not qualified or emotionally equipped to handle a dog with that kind of sophisticated training. When commands are given lackadaisically or, worse still, omitted at the proper moment, the situation becomes hazardous, especially in a family with children.

The Akita's natural temperament can be said to be 50% gentleness, 25% aggressiveness and the remaining 25% like a piece of clay that the owner can mold to his liking. The average layman, not too familar with dogs in general, is quick to misinterpret, criticize or take too much for granted. Halftruths and ignorance create confusion, resulting in 'old wives tales' and false assumptions, harmful to any breed. Therefore, it pays lasting dividends to learn something about its characteristics and idiosyncrasies first. Get to know something about the breed before

Facing page: As a companion and protector, the Akita is invaluable—as a rule, he is responsive and courageous.

you fall in love with that cuddly-bear Akita puppy.

Since the Akita matures into a large dog weighing one hundred pounds and more, he is hardly suitable as an apartment dweller. He will be happiest in a home with a fenced-in yard to run and play as long as he is also allowed to be a house dog and participate in the family's activities. Extremely affectionate by nature, he needs this closeness with his owner but remains aloof with any stranger. With that unfathomable oriental gaze, he appears to be watching the newcomer as if to divine his intentions.

A typical Akita trait is his endless curiosity. When particularly affectionate, he will gently 'carry' the owner's arm or hand and to his animal buddies he gives tender 'love-nibbles.'

Many a first time Akita owner is perplexed by the breed's apparent lack of vocalizing. He never is an inveterate barker, but when he does sound off, it pays to pay attention and investigate. Most dogs growl a warning. The Akita remains silent but if you know your dog, you will observe how the sweet expression he usually carries, changes to one of an almost baleful look. It plainly says: '*Watch out!*' and only a hapless fool would ignore that look.

Never underestimate your Akita's protective instincts. In one instance, one owner's Akita

accidentally got out while she was at work. A neighbor managed to coax the dog back inside but when she decided she might as well babysit with him till the owners returned, he refused to let her cross the threshold. In another

Restless or indecisive, this puppy is surely enjoying his moment in the great outdoors.

instance, a plumber was called to a home for some kitchen sink repairs. After watching the proceedings for a while, the owner's Akita decided to remove the man's tools, one by one. After that he gently took one of the plumber's ankles in his mouth. The plumber's eyes bulged with terror and his squawk for help was

A Description of the Breed

almost lost in his throat. Finally released from the canine shackle, he whispered a request that the Akita be removed so he could get on with his work. Neither of the dogs displayed the slightest viciousness; they simply took care of the situation in their own individual ways.

DIFFERENT STRAINS

There are two strains of Akita: the *Ichinoseki*, short and compact with heavy bone and the *Dewa*, taller, medium boned and of medium body by comparison.

There are few true representatives of either one of these strains. All have been crossed and recrossed in an effort to improve the Akita as a breed. However, whether the Ichinoseki or Dewa is more evident in any one individual, the Akita is definitely an Akita and incomparable to any other breed.

The most famous of Akita ancestors in Japan was the one and only Kongo-Go. He was

Akita puppies, like most puppies, are energetic and enjoy the attention of their human comrades.

considered the ultimate prototype of the Dewa line. In most American pedigrees, Kongo appears at least in the fourth and fifth generations. In fact, following World War II, he and his progeny so dominated that someone commented: "If it is not from Kongo-Go, it is not an Akita Dog." His type is no longer representative of the Akita in Japan today, but rather some excellent specimens of the Ichinoseki represent the modern day Japanese Akita.

Kongo-Go was owned by Mr. Heihacki Hashimoto who died March 7, 1977. Mr. Hashimoto will be remembered best, perhaps, for having owned the most famous Akita of all time. The years of Kongo's reign and those few years following were to be the "Golden Age" for Akitas in the United States. His descendants became the foundation stock of American breeders who took the Akita to their hearts in the mid-1950s. It is safe to say that the development of today's Akitas in this country was rooted in Japanese dogs of the 40s, 50s and early 60s. At that time the large, massive dog was king pin in his native land.

THE AKITA ALLIANCE

There is today a growing alliance between Japanese and American breeders. Unbiased opinions are exchanged and comparisons made; not as a

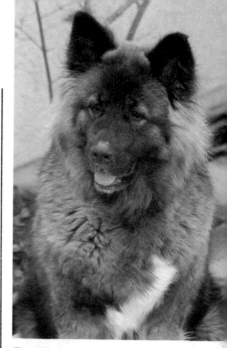

The Akita's warm and versatile personality has contributed to the breed's growing popularity in the United States.

criticism but to uphold the highest standard of perfection for the breed. Every year Don and Twyla Lusk, editors and publishers of *The Akita Journal* and owners of the Arashi Hoshi Akitas, take a trip to Japan to nurture this progressive alliance. They talk with breeders in that country and visit the Headquarters Shows. They return with a wealth of information that is passed on to the Akita fancy in this country. As a token of appreciation and sincere friendship, the Lusks were given a gorgeous red-golden (sesame) Akita puppy during their 1977 visit. The dog's name is

A Description of the Breed

Shinbei which, translated, means "from the heart to America," certainly a meaningful sentiment to continue the friendship that began with Helen Keller.

JAPANESE OBSERVATIONS

Shinbei, incidentally, is the typical representative of the Akita in Japan today. Both his grandsire and granddam are *Meiyoshi* winners (the highest award given at a Headquarters Show).

Conversations and discussions with Japanese breeders have disclosed some interesting observations regarding the Akita in America today. These are not meant as criticism but should be taken as friendly advice. One comment is that more attention should be paid to breed the typical Akita head with the ears set somewhat to the side and pointing slightly forward. Smallish and of a definite triangular shape, they should not be set too high on the head, nor be long and pointed like the German Shepherd Dog's. It is that quite unique earset, combined with the deep-set oriental eyes, that give the Akita that expression of mystery and sweetness, and an air of aloofness.

According to one Japanese judge, the greatest difference between Japanese- and American-bred Akitas is that the latter still show much evidence of the Dewa strain.

Further comments concern a certain lack of spirit and of presence which is characteristic of the breed. There should never be

These two Akitas enjoy the opportunity to roughhouse in the backyard.

Potential dog owners should be aware that a dog as large as the Akita will need a substantial amount of space in which to exercise.

anything 'wishy-washy' about an Akita. Also there seems to be a lack of firmness and discipline on the part of owners inclined to 'baby' their Akitas. Many are overweight and in soft condition. Some are either too shy or too aggressive when there should be a tolerable balance. The Akita should carry his bushy tail proudly and naturally over the back and not have it positioned, or worse, held there. Japanese handlers never touch their dogs in the ring. The lead is held high with several feet between dog and handler giving the impression that the dog is straining forward, looking alert and full of spirit. Of course, one has to take into consideration that our conformation rings are much smaller and, with a large breed, get crowded. However, as mentioned before, the above are simply views and comparisons and, on the whole, Japanese judges who come to the U.S. are impressed with the overall quality of American Akitas. But to pay close attention to emotional and spiritual qualities, as well as general appearance, can only

benefit the breed.

Maybe we are a bit 'soft' with our dogs and spoil them more than we should, or more than is good for them. Especially when yours is a house pet, spoiling them is an irresistible temptation.

To amplify the points mentioned earlier, American breeders are duly concerned about the closing of registrations to imported Akitas. It is a regrettable step taken by the AKC and, it is hoped that, in the future there will be a reversal in order to retain the desirable qualities found in Akitas in Japan today.

Since the Akita Club of America was founded in 1956, the breed has made great strides and much credit is due American breeders. However, and as is the case with other imported breeds, the infusion of valuable bloodlines is important to uphold the quality and characteristics as set down by the standard of perfection as well as further purposeful progress in the breeding of these fine animals.

STANDARD FOR THE BREED

In order to preserve the various desired characteristics of a breed, a standard of perfection is issued by the dog-registering

Facing page: *Undeniably, the Akita is a very handsome and impressive dog, well-deserving of the praise and popularity he enjoys, and much more.*

organizations around the world. This breed standard of perfection indicates what the ideal specimen of that breed should look like. Each dog-registering organization has its own set of standards, one for each of the breeds it recognizes; however, these standards may vary, in the way they are worded, from registry to registry and from country to country. Following is an example of a breed standard for the Akita to provide you with an idea of what a standard looks like, what it includes, and what it attempts to accomplish.

General Appearance: Large, powerful, alert, with much substance and heavy bone. The broad head, forming a blunt triangle, with deep muzzle, small eyes and erect ears carried forward in line with back of neck is characteristic of the breed. The large, curled tail, balancing the broad head, is also characteristic of the breed.

Head: Massive though in balance with body; free of wrinkles when at ease. Skull, flat between ears and broad; jaws, square and powerful with minimal dewlap. Head forms a blunt triangle when viewed from above. **Fault:** *Narrow or snipy head.*

Muzzle: Broad and full. Distance from nose to stop is distance from stop to occiput as two is to three. Stop, well-defined but not too abrupt. A shallow furrow extends well up forehead.

Nose: Broad and black. Liver permitted on white Akitas, but black always preferred. **Disqualification:** *Butterfly nose or total lack of pigmentation on nose.*

Ears: The ears of the Akita are characteristic of the breed. They are strongly erect and small in relation to rest of head. If ear is folded forward for measuring length, tip will touch upper eye rim. Ears are triangular, slightly rounded at tip, wide at base, set wide on head but not too low, and carried slightly forward over eyes in line with back of neck. **Disqualification:** *Dropped or broken ears.*

Eyes: Dark brown, small, deep-set and triangular in shape. Eye rims, black and tight.

Lips and Tone: Lips, black and not pendulous; tongue, pink.

Teeth: Strong with scissors bite preferred, but level bite acceptable. **Disqualification:** *Noticeably undershot or overshot.*

Neck: Thick and muscular; comparatively short, widening gradually toward shoulders. A pronounced crest blends in with base of skull.

Body: Longer than high. Chest, wide and deep; depth of chest is one-half height of dog at shoulder. Ribs, well-sprung, brisket, well-developed. Level back with firmly muscled loin and moderate tuck-up. Skin pliant but not loose. **Faults:** *Light bone, rangy body.*

Tail: Large and full, set high and carried over back or against flank in a three-quarter, full, or double curl, always dipping to or below level of back. On a three-quarter curl, tip drops well down flank. Root, large and strong. Tail bone reaches hock when let down. Hair, coarse, straight and full, with no appearance of a plume. **Disqualification:** *Sickle or uncurled tail.*

Forequarters: Shoulders, strong and powerful with moderate layback. Forelegs, heavy boned and straight as viewed from front. Angle of pastern, 15 degrees forward from vertical. **Faults:** *Elbows. in or out: loose shoulders.*

Hindquarters: Width, muscular development are comparable to forequarters. Upper thighs, well-developed. Stifle, moderately bent and hocks well let down, turning neither in nor out. Dewclaws on front legs, generally not removed; dewclaws on hind legs, generally removed. Feet, cat feet, well-knuckled up with thick pads. Feet, straight ahead.

Coat: Double-coated. Undercoat, thick, soft, dense and shorter than outer coat. Outer coat, straight, harsh and standing somewhat off body. Hair on head,

Facing page: *It is truly a wonder how an Akita mother is able to handle a litter as large as this one—one might think that the situation would frequently get "out of paw."*

Small in relation to the rest of the head, the Akita's ears, erect and alert, are prominent in this head study of the breed.

legs, and ears, short. Length of hair at withers and rump approximately two inches, which is slightly longer than on rest of body, except tail, where coat is longest and most profuse. **Fault:** *Any indication of ruff or feathering.*

Color: Any color including white, brindle, or pinto. Colors are brilliant and clear and markings are well-balanced, with or without mask or blaze. White Akitas have no mask. Pinto has a white background with large, evenly placed patches covering head and more than one-third of body.

Undercoat may be a different color from outer coat.

Gait: Brisk and powerful with strides of moderate length. Back remains strong, firm and level. Rear legs move in line with front legs.

Size: Males, 26 to 28 inches at the withers; bitches, 24 to 26 inches. **Disqualification:** *Dogs, under 25 inches; bitches, under 23 inches.*

Temperament: Alert and responsive, dignified and courageous. Aggressive toward other dogs.

Selecting Your Dog

Now that you have decided which dog breed suits your needs, your lifestyle, and your own temperament, there will be much to consider before you make your final purchase. Buying a puppy on impulse may only cause heartbreak later on; it makes better sense to put some real thought into your canine investment, especially since it is likely that he will share many happy years with you. Which individual will you choose as your adoring companion? Ask yourself some questions as you analyze your needs and preferences for a dog, read all that you can about your particular breed, and visit as many dog shows as possible. At the shows you will be surrounded by people who can give you all the details about the breed you are interested in buying. Decide if you want a household pet, a dog for breeding, or a show dog. Would you prefer a male or female? Puppy or adult?

If you buy from a breeder, ask him to help you with your decision. When you have settled on the dog you want, discuss with him the dog's temperament, the animal's positive and negative aspects, any health problems it might have, its feeding and grooming requirements, and whether the dog has been immunized. Reputable breeders will be willing to answer any questions you might have that pertain to the dog you have selected, and often they will make themselves available if you call for advice or if you encounter problems after you've made your purchase.

In choosing your new Akita, be sure that he is of sound disposition and of agreeable temperament.

A bit too big?
A little **too** small.
Too fuzzy for me!
Too fat to crawl.

Before you wrap it tight
And crate it home,
Behold its appetite
And room to roam.

A sloppy yap, a barking slur,
Puppy eyes to be let free,
A him? a her? an unmarked cur,
Let's pout to see its pedigree.

The perfect pet quest:
Which pup for me is best?

ANDREW DE PRISCO

Most breeders want to see their dogs placed in loving, responsible homes; they are careful about who buys their animals. So as the dog's new owner, prepare yourself for some interrogation from the breeder.

WHERE TO BUY

You can choose among several places to buy your dog. Many people think of their local pet shop as the first source for buying a puppy, and very often they're right; you should remember, however, that a pet shop cannot possibly stock all breeds of dog. If your pet shop does not carry the type of dog you desire, there are other places to look. One is a kennel whose business is breeding show-quality dogs; such kennels may have extra pups for sale. Another source is the one-dog owner who wants to sell the puppies from an occasional litter to pay the expenses of his small-scale breeding operation. To find such kennels and part-time breeders and hobbyists, check the classified section of your local newspaper or look in your telephone directory.

Whichever source you choose, you can usually tell in a very short time whether the puppies will make healthy and happy pets. If they are clean, plump, and lively, they are probably in good health. At the breeder's you will have the advantage of seeing the puppies' dam and perhaps their sire and other relatives. Remember that the mother, having just raised a demanding family, may not be looking her best; but if she is sturdy, friendly, and well-mannered, her puppies should be too. If you feel that something is lacking in the care or condition of the dogs, it is better to look elsewhere than to buy hastily and regret it afterward. Buy a healthy dog with a good disposition, one that has been

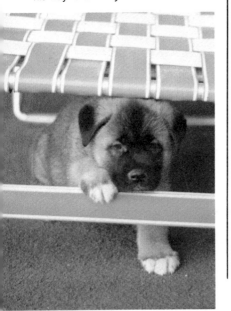

Your new Akita may be so anxious to get to know you that he may go out of his way to attract your attention!

As graceful and affectionate as he is strong and protective, the Akita is one of the most beloved dogs in the canine world.

properly socialized and likes being around people.

If you cannot find the dog you want locally, write to the secretary of the national breed club or kennel club and ask for names of breeders near you or to whom you can write for information. Puppies are often shipped, sight unseen, from reputable breeders. In these instances, pictures and pedigree information are usually sent beforehand to help you decide.

Breeders can supply you with further details and helpful guidance, if you require it. Many breed clubs provide a puppy referral service, so you may want to look into this before making your final decision.

PET OR SHOW DOG

Conscientious breeders strive to maintain those desirable qualities in their breed. At the same time, they are always working to improve on what they have already achieved, and they do this by referring to the breed standard of perfection. The standard describes the ideal dog, and those animals that come close to the ideal are generally selected as show

Owners of purebred dogs too often forget that all breeds of dog are interrelated. The ancient canine that is the believed ancestor of all dogs is known as Tomarctus. As packs traveled and inhabited various lands, types evolved through the process of adaptation. Later, as dogs and man joined forces, type became further diversified. This chart sketches one commonly accepted theory of the domesticated dog's development. Where does your dog fit in? With a few exceptions, dogs evolve or change as a result of a specific functional need.

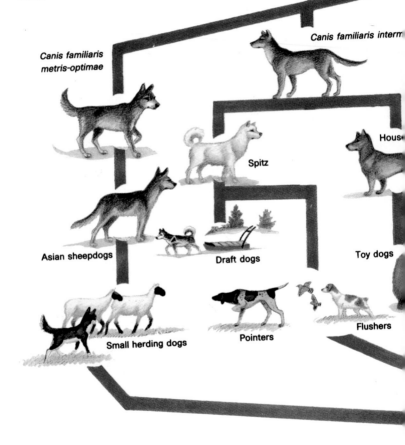

Canis familiaris interm

Canis familiaris
metris-optimae

Spitz

Hous

Asian sheepdogs

Draft dogs

Toy dogs

Small herding dogs

Pointers

Flushers

Tomarctus

Canis familiaris leineri

Canis familiaris inostranzewi

Russian Tracker

Molossian

Scenthounds

hound
otypes

Mastiffs

Sighthounds

Terriers

Bulldogs

Retrievers

Large herding dogs

stock; those that do not are culled and sold as pets. Keep in mind that pet-quality purebred dogs are in no way less healthy or attractive than show-quality specimens. It's just that the pet may have undesirable features (such as ears that are too large or eyes that are the wrong color for its breed) which would be faults in the show ring. Often these so-called ''flaws'' are detectable only by experienced breeders or show judges. Naturally the more perfect animal, in terms of its breed standard, will cost more—even though he seems almost identical to his pet-quality littermate.

If you think you may eventually want to show your dog or raise a litter of puppies, by all means buy the best you can afford. You will save expense and disappointment later on. However, if the puppy is strictly to be a pet for the children, or a companion for you, you can afford to look for a bargain. The pup which is not show material, or the older pup for which there is often less demand, or the grown dog which is not being used for breeding are occasionally available and offer opportunities to save money. Remember that your initial investment may be a bargain, but it takes good food and care— and plenty of both—to raise a healthy, vigorous puppy through its adulthood.

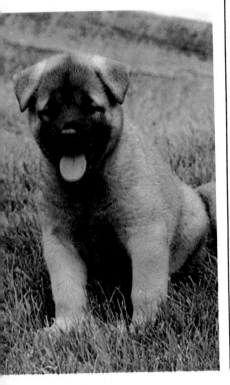

Even as a small puppy, the Akita demonstrates an unusually high level of self-control and dignity.

Facing page: *The breed's powerful and imposing appearance is undoubtedly reinforced by its bear-like resemblance. Owner, Louise D. Beakes.*

The price you pay for your dog is little compared to the love and devotion he will return over the many years he'll be with you. With proper care and affection, your pup should live to a ripe old age; thanks to modern veterinary science and improvements in canine nutrition, dogs today are better maintained and live longer. It is not uncommon to see dogs living well into their teens.

Generally speaking, small dogs live longer than big ones. With love and the proper care any dog will live to its optimum age. Many persons, however, opt for a particular breed because of its proven longevity. This, of course, is purely a personal decision.

MALE OR FEMALE

Let us first disregard the usual generalizations and misconceptions applied to male vs. female dogs and consider the practical concerns. If you intend to show your new dog, a male will likely closer adhere to the

Size variation in the dog family is extreme. The consideration of size must be a high priority when choosing a breed. The amount of housing, exercise, and food required, as well as the animal's lifespan are just some of the factors involved.

breed standard, though ring competition for males is stiffer. A female chosen to show cannot be spayed and the owner must contend with the bitch's heat period. If it is solely a pet—and pet animals should *not* be bred—castration or spaying is necessary. Neutered pets have longer lifespans and have a decreased risk of cancer. Males are more economical to neuter than are females. You might also consider that females are generally smaller than males, easier to housetrain, may be more family-oriented and protective of home and property. Any dog will roam—male or female—castration will not affect roaming in most cases. Males are larger and stronger, proving better guard-dog candidates. Of course, a dog of either sex, if properly trained, can make a charming, reliable, and loving pet. Male vs. female is chiefly a matter of personal preference—go with your first instinct.

ADULT OR PUP

Whether to buy a grown dog or a young puppy is another question. It is surely an undeniable pleasure to watch your dog grow from a lively pup to a mature, dignified dog. If you don't have the time to spend on the more frequent meals, housebreaking, and other training a puppy needs in order to become a dog you can be

Life Expectancy	
Dog's Age in Years	Comparative Human Age in Years
1	15
2	24
3	28
4	32
5	36
6	40
7	44
8	48
9	52
10	56
11	60
12	64
13	68
14	72
15	76
16	80
17	84
18	88
19	92
20	96
21	100

This chart is designed to provide a comparative view of ages between a dog and its human counterpart. Necessarily it is an oversimplification since larger breeds often have shorter lifespans than do average or medium-sized dogs; likewise working dogs may tend to live shorter lives than the easygoing pet dog. These factors, and many others, must be taken into account when considering this chart.

proud of, then choose an older, partly-trained adolescent or a grown dog. If you want a show dog, remember that no one, not even an expert, can predict with one hundred percent accuracy what a puppy will be like when he grows up. The dog may seem to exhibit show potential *most* of the time, but six months is the earliest age for the would-be exhibitor to select a prospect and know that its future is in the show ring.

If you have a small child, it is best to get a puppy big enough to defend itself, one not less than four or five months old.

Older children will enjoy playing with and helping to take care of a baby pup; but at less than four months, a puppy wants to do little else but eat and sleep, and he must be protected from teasing and overtiring. You cannot expect a very young child to understand that a puppy is a fragile living being; to the youngster he is a toy like his

The Akita is a dog of placid and disciplined demeanor. His calmness and unshatterable control are unmatched by any other breed.

Like all puppies, the Akita puppy spends a good amount of time resting and enjoying the carefree days of puppyhood.

stuffed dog. Children, therefore, must learn how to handle and care for their young pets.

We recommend you start with a puppy so that you can raise and train it according to the rules you have established in your own home. While a dog is young, its behavior can be more easily shaped by the owner, whereas an older dog , although trainable, may be a bit set in his ways.

WHAT TO LOOK FOR IN A PUPPY

In choosing a puppy, assuming that it comes from healthy, well-bred parents, look for one that is friendly and outgoing. The biggest pup in the litter is apt to be somewhat coarse as a grown dog, while the appealing "runt of the litter" may turn out to be a timid shadow—or have a Napoleonic complex! If you want a show dog and have no experience in choosing a prospect, study the breed standard and listen carefully to the breeder on the finer points of show conformation. A breeder's prices will be in accord with his puppies' expected worth, and he will be honest with you about each pup's potential because it is to his own advantage. He wants his top-quality show puppies placed in the public eye to reflect glory on him—and to attract future buyers. Why should he sell a potential show champion to someone who just wants a pet?

Now that you have paid your money and made your choice, you are ready to depart with puppy, papers, and instructions. Make sure that you know the youngster's feeding routine, and take along some of his food. For the trip home, place him in a comfortable, sturdy carrier. Do not drive home with a puppy on your lap! If you'll be travelling for a few hours, at the very least bring along a bottle of water from the breeder and a small water dish.

PEDIGREE AND REGISTRATION

Owners of puppies are often misled by sellers with such ruses as leading the owner to believe his dog is something special. The term *pedigree papers* is quite different from the term *registration papers.* A pedigree is nothing more than a statement made by the breeder of the dog;

If you have never been to a dog show, whether you're interested in show dogs or not, by all means—Go! An all-breed dog show will give you hands-on experience with different breeds of dog, the chance to meet their owners and breeders, and the answers to many of your questions.

Our Dog's *Pedigree*

REGISTERED NAME	INDIVIDUAL REG. NO.	REG. LITTER NO.	CALL NAME
BREED	SEX	BORN	COLOR AND MARKINGS
BREEDER	ADDRESS	CITY	STATE
LITTER IDENTIFICATION	SOLD TO	ADDRESS

PARENTS   GRANDPARENTS   GREAT GRANDPARENTS   GREAT GREAT GRANDPARENTS

Pedigree papers can trace a dog's lineage back several generations. They do not, however, guarantee that a puppy is purebred, healthy or sound.

and it is written on special pedigree blanks, which are readily available from any pet shop or breed club, with the names of several generations from which the new puppy comes. It records your puppy's ancestry and other important data, such as the pup's date of birth, its breed, its sex, its sire and dam, its breeder's name and address, and so on. If your dog has had purebred champions in his background, then the pedigree papers are valuable as evidence of the good breeding behind your dog; but if the names on the pedigree paper are meaningless, then so is the paper itself. Just because a dog has a pedigree doesn't necessarily mean he is registered with a kennel club.

Registration papers from the American Kennel Club or the United Kennel Club in the United States or The Kennel Club of Great Britain attest to the fact that the mother and father of your puppy were purebred dogs of the breed represented by your puppy and that they were registered with a particular club. Normally every registered dog also has a complete pedigree available. Registration papers, which you receive when you buy a puppy, merely enable you to register your puppy. Usually the breeder has registered only the litter, so it is the new owner's responsibility to register and name an individual pup. The papers should be filled out and sent to the appropriate address printed on the application, along with the fee required for the registration. A certificate of registration will then be sent to you.

Pedigree and registration, by the way, have nothing to do with licensing, which is a local regulation applying to purebred and mongrel alike. Find out what the local ordinance is in your town or city and how it applies to your dog; then buy a license and keep it on your dog's collar for identification.

Akitas may come in a large variety of colors; these two unmasked pups brilliantly reveal the two ends of the color spectrum.

The New Family Member

A basket ot abounding good luck, warmth, and affection—a welcome bundle to any home!

At long last, the day you have all been waiting for, your new puppy will make its grand entrance into your home. Before you bring your companion to its new residence, however, you must plan carefully for its arrival. Keep in mind that the puppy will need time to adjust to life with a different owner. He may seem a bit apprehensive about the strange surroundings in which he finds himself, having spent the first few weeks of life with his dam and littermates, but in a couple of days, with love and patience on your part, the transition will be complete.

First impressions are important, especially from the puppy's point of view, and these may very well set the pattern of his future relationship with you. You must be consistent in the

The puppy's bed will provide a place of refuge and privacy. Make sure that the puppy's toilet needs have been met before sending him to bed for the night.

way you handle your pet so that he learns what is expected of him. He must come to trust and respect you as his keeper and master. Provide him with proper care and attention, and you will be rewarded with a loyal companion for many years. Considering the needs of your puppy and planning ahead will surely make the change from his former home to his new one easier.

ADVANCE PREPARATION

In preparing for your puppy's arrival, perhaps more important than anything else is to find out from the seller how the pup was maintained. What brand of food was offered and when and how often was the puppy fed? Has

BASIC PUPPY NEEDS

- Canned and dry food/diet schedule
- Feeding and water bowls
- Carrying/sleeping crate
- Bed
- Collar and leash
- Grooming supplies (brushes, shampoo, etc.)
- Outdoor lead and/or pen
- Muzzle/first-aid kit
- Flea collar and preparations
- Safe chew products (Nylabone®, Gumabone®)
- Edible chew products (treats/rewards)

the pup been housebroken; if so, what method was employed? Attempt to continue whatever routine was started by the person from whom you bought your puppy; then, gradually, you can make those changes that suit you and your lifestyle. If, for example, the puppy has been paper trained, plan to stock up on newspaper. Place this newspaper toilet facility in a selected spot so that your puppy learns to use the designated area as his "bathroom." And keep on hand a supply of the dog food to which he is accustomed, as a sudden switch to new food could cause digestive upsets.

Another consideration is sleeping and resting quarters. Be sure to supply a dog bed for your pup, and introduce him to his special cozy corner so that he

This chart lists some of the many items that the dog owner should have on hand before he brings home his new charge.

knows where to retire when he feels like taking a snooze. You'll need to buy a collar (or harness) and leash, a safe chew item (such as Nylabone® or Gumabone®), and a few grooming tools as well. A couple of sturdy feeding dishes, one for food and one for water, will be needed; and it will be necessary, beforehand, to set up a feeding station.

FINDING A VETERINARIAN
An important part of your preparations should include finding a local veterinarian who can provide quality health care in the form of routine check-ups,

The New Family Member

inoculations, and prompt medical attention in case of illness or an emergency. Find out if the animal you have selected has been vaccinated against canine diseases, and make certain you secure all health certificates at the time of purchase. This information will be valuable to your veterinarian, who will want to know the puppy's complete medical history. Incidentally, don't wait until your puppy becomes sick before you seek the services of a vet; make an appointment for your pup before or soon after he takes up residence with you so that he starts out with a clean bill of health in his new home.

CHILDREN AND PUPPIES

Prepare the young members of the household on pet care. Children should learn not only to love their charges but to respect them and treat them with the consideration one would give all living things. It must be emphasized to youngsters that the puppy has certain needs, just as humans have, and all family members must take an active role in ensuring that these needs are met. Someone must feed the puppy. Someone must walk him a couple of times a day or clean up after him if he is trained to relieve himself on newspaper. Someone must groom his coat, clean his ears, and clip his nails from time to time. Someone

must see to it that the puppy gets sufficient exercise and attention each day.

A child who has a pet to care for learns responsibility; nonetheless, parental guidance is an essential part of his learning experience. Many a child has been known to "love a pet to death," squeezing and hugging the animal in ways which are irritating or even painful. Others have been found guilty of teasing, perhaps unintentionally, and disturbing their pet while the animal is eating or resting. One must teach a child, therefore, when and how to gently stroke and fondle a puppy. In time, the child can learn how to carefully pick up and handle the pup. A dog should always be supported with both hands, *not* lifted by the scruff of the neck. One hand placed under the chest, between the front legs, and the other hand supporting the dog's rear end will be comfortable and will restrain the animal as you hold and carry him. Always demonstrate to children the proper way to lift a dog.

BE A GOOD NEIGHBOR

For the sake of your dog's safety and well being, don't allow him to wander onto the property of others. Keep him confined at all times to your own yard or indoors where he won't become a nuisance. Consider what

The unmistakably sincere expression of the Akita coupled with his graceful, cat-like mannerisms make him a truly unique and gentle companion. Owner, Brian Douglas.

The New Family Member

Clockwise from upper right: *pokeweed, jimson weed, foxglove, and yew*. If ingested, any toxic plant can be dangerous to your dog.

Rover will not be harmed if you follow my instructions

AMF

Dog theft is not an uncommon event. Dognappers will steal either a purebred or mongrel puppy so all owners must always be wary.

dangers lie ahead for an unleashed dog that has total freedom of the great outdoors, particularly when he is unsupervised by his master. There are cars and trucks to dodge on the streets and highways. There are stray animals with which to wrangle. There are poisons all around, such as car antifreeze in driveways or toxic plants and shrubs, which, if swallowed, could prove fatal. There are dognappers and sadistic people who may steal or bring harm to your beloved pet. In short, there are all sorts of nasty things waiting to hurt him. Did you know that if your dog consumes rotting garbage, there is the possibility he could go into shock or even die? And are you aware that a dog left to roam in a wooded area or field could become infected with any number of parasites if he plays with or ingests some small prey, such as a rabbit, that might be carrying these parasitic organisms? A thorn from a rosebush imbedded in the dog's foot pad, tar from a newly paved road stuck to his coat, and a wound inflicted by a wild animal all can be avoided if you take the precaution of keeping your dog in a safe enclosure where he will be protected from such dangers. Don't let your dog run loose; he is likely to stray from home and get into all sorts of trouble.

The New Family Member

GETTING ACQUAINTED

Plan to bring your new pet home in the morning so that by nightfall he will have had some time to become acquainted with you and his new environment. Avoid introducing the pup to the family around holiday time, since all of the extra excitement will only add to the confusion and frighten him. Let the puppy enter your home on a day when the

Resist the temptation to handle him too much during these first few days. And, if there are other dogs or animals around the house, make certain all are properly introduced. If you observe fighting among the animals, or some other problem, you may have to separate all parties until they learn to accept one another. Remember that neglecting your other pets while

routine is normal. For those people who work during the week, a Saturday morning is an ideal time to bring the puppy to his new home; this way he has the entire weekend to make adjustments before being left alone for a few hours, come Monday morning.

Let the puppy explore, under your watchful eye of course, and let him come to know his new home without stress and fear.

In some countries, the Akita is used as a sled dog—the powerful build of these dogs make them ideal for a variety of the tasks in which other canines have already excelled.

Facing page: *Throughout the centuries, the Akita has proven to be a most reliable protector and worker as well as a loyal and loving companion. No matter which role the Akita is expected to fulfill, he does so with dignity and conviction. Owners, Joel and Jeanette Ward.*

showering the new puppy with extra attention will only cause animosity and jealousy. Make an effort to pay special attention to the other animals as well.

On that eventful first night, try not to give in and let the puppy sleep with you; otherwise, this could become a difficult habit to break. Let him cry and whimper, even if it means a night of restlessness for the entire family. Some people have had success with putting a doll or a hot water bottle wrapped in a towel in the puppy's bed as a surrogate mother, while others have placed a ticking alarm clock in the bed to simulate the heartbeat of the pup's dam and littermates. Remember that this furry little fellow is used to the warmth and security of his mother and siblings, so the adjustment to sleeping alone will take time. Select a location away from drafts and away from the feeding station for placement of his dog bed. Keep in mind, also, that the bed should be roomy enough for him to stretch out in; as he grows older, you may need to supply a larger one.

Prior to the pup's arrival, set up his room and partition it the way you would to keep an infant out of a particular area. You may want to keep his bed, his feeding station, and his toilet area all in the same room—in separate locations—or you may want to set the feeding station up in your kitchen, where meals for all family members are served. Whatever you decide, do it ahead of time so you will have that much less to worry about when your puppy finally moves in with you.

Above all else, be patient with your puppy as he adjusts to life in his new home. If you purchase a pup that is not housebroken, you will have to spend time with the dog—just as you would with a small child—until he develops proper toilet habits. Even a housebroken puppy may feel nervous in strange new surroundings and have an occasional accident. Praise and encouragement will elicit far better results than punishment or scolding. Remember that your puppy wants nothing more than to please you, thus he is anxious to learn the behavior that is required of him.

Feeding Requirements

Perhaps more than any other single aspect of your dog's development, proper feeding requires an educated and responsible dog owner. The importance of nutrition on your dog's bone and muscle growth cannot be overemphasized.

Soon after your puppy comes to live with you, he will need to be fed. Remember to ask the seller what foods were given to the youngster and stay with that diet for a while. It is important for the puppy to keep eating and to avoid skipping a meal, so entice him with the food to which he is accustomed. If you prefer to switch to some other brand of dog food, each day begin to add small quantities of the new brand to the usual food offering. Make the portions of the new food progressively larger until the pup is weaned from his former diet.

What should you feed the puppy and how often? His diet is really quite simple and relatively inexpensive to prepare. Puppies need to be fed small portions at frequent intervals, since they are growing and their activity level is high. You must ensure that your pup gains weight steadily; with an adult dog, however, growth slows down and weight must be regulated to prevent obesity and a host of other problems. At one time, it was thought that home-cooked meals were the answer, with daily rations of meat,

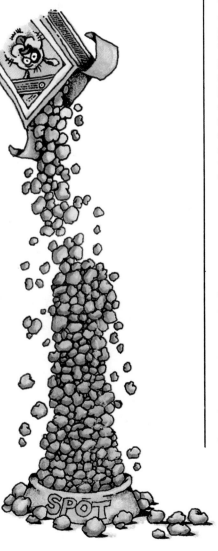

Choosing a quality dog food from your pet shop is easy—deciding how much to feed may not be as straightforward. Feedings must always be carefully monitored.

Feeding Requirements

vegetables, egg yolk, cereal, cheese, brewer's yeast, and vitamin supplements. With all of the nutritionally complete commercial dog food products readily available, these time-consuming preparations really are unnecessary now. A great deal of money and research has resulted in foods that we can serve our dogs with confidence and pride; and most of these commercial foods have been developed along strict guidelines according to the size, weight, and age of your dog. These products are reasonably priced, easy to find, and convenient to store.

THE PUPPY'S MEALS

After a puppy has been fully weaned from its mother until approximately three months of age, it needs to be fed four times a day. In the morning and evening offer kibble (dog meal) soaked in hot water or broth, to which you have added some canned meat-based food or fresh raw meat cut into small chunks. At noon and bedtime feed him a bit of kibble or whole-grain cereal moistened with milk (moistening, by the way, makes the food easier to digest, since dogs don't typically chew their food). From three to six months, increase the portion size and

This pile of playful Akita puppies enthusiastically await their next meal. Young puppies need to be fed up to four times a day (in small quantities).

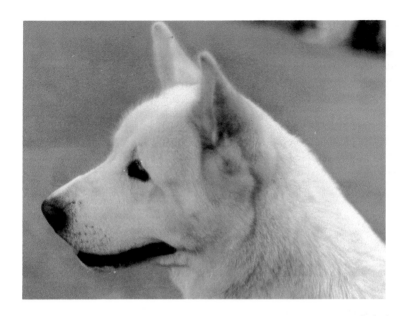

The white Akita is a striking and beautiful dog—notice it is the one Akita that does not have a mask.

offer just three meals—one milk and two meat. At six months, two meals are sufficient; at one year, a single meal can be given, supplemented with a few dry biscuits in the morning and evening. During the colder months, especially if your dog is active, you might want to mix in some wheat germ oil or corn oil or bacon drippings with the meal to add extra calories. Remember to keep a bowl of cool, fresh water on hand always to help your dog regulate its body temperature and to aid in digestion.

From one year on, you may continue feeding the mature dog a single meal (in the evening, perhaps, when you have your supper), or you may prefer to divide this meal in two, offering half in the morning and the other half at night. Keep in mind that while puppies require foods in small chunks, or nuggets, older dogs can handle larger pieces of food at mealtime. Discuss your dog's feeding schedule with your veterinarian; he can make suggestions about the right diet for your particular canine friend.

COMPARISON SHOPPING
With so many fine dog-food products on the market today, there is something for

everyone's pet. You may want to serve dry food "as is" or mix it with warm water or broth. Perhaps you'll choose to combine dry food with fresh or canned preparations. Some canned foods contain all meat, but they are not complete; others are mixtures of meat and grains, which have been fortified with additional nutrients to make them more complete and balanced. There are also various packaged foods that can be served alone or as supplements and that can be left out for a few hours without spoiling. This self-feeding method, which works well for dogs that are not prone to weight problems, allows the animal to serve himself whenever he feels hungry. Many people who work during the day find these dry or semi-moist rations convenient to use, and these foods are great to bring along if you travel with your dog.

Be sure to read the labels carefully before you make your dog-food purchases. Most

Feeder bins are used by many kennel owners as well as pet owners. These devices help to conveniently store and distribute dry foods in a sanitary, efficient way.

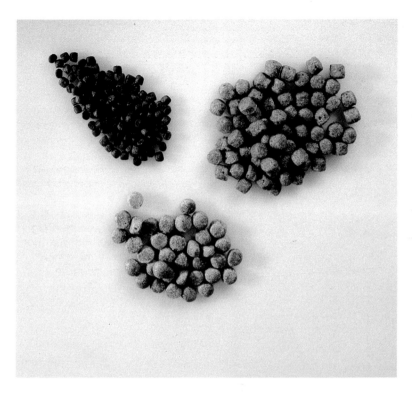

Pet shops offer a variety of dry kibbles. Though the nutritional values of these foods are essentially equivalent, compare the manufacturer's labels.

reputable pet-food manufacturers list the ingredients and the nutritional content right on the can or package. Instructions are usually included so that you will know how much to feed your dog to keep him thriving and in top condition. A varied, well-balanced diet that supplies the proper amounts of protein, carbohydrate, fat, vitamins, minerals, and water is important to keep your puppy healthy and to guarantee his normal development. Adjustments to the diet can be made, under your veterinarian's supervision, according to the individual puppy, his rate of growth, his activity level, and so on. Liquid or powder vitamin and mineral supplements, or those in tablet form, are available and can be given if you need to feel certain that the diet is balanced.

A dog of incomparable courage and strength, the Akita is a fearless and aggressive hunter. Owner, Gayle Pierce.

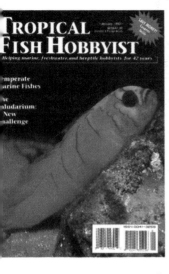

Since 1952, *Tropical Fish Hobbyist* has been the source of accurate, up-to-the-minute, and fascinating information on every facet of the aquarium hobby. Join the more than 50,000 devoted readers world-wide who wouldn't miss a single issue.

Subscribe right now so you don't miss a single copy!

DEVELOPING GOOD EATING HABITS

Try to serve your puppy his meals at the same time each day and in the same location so that he will get used to his daily routine and develop good eating habits. A bit of raw egg, cottage cheese, or table scraps (leftover food from your own meals) can be offered from time to time; but never accustom your dog to eating human "junk food." Cake, candy, chocolate, soda, and other snack foods are for people, not dogs. Besides, these foods provide only "empty" calories that your pet doesn't need if he is to stay healthy. Avoid offering spicy, fried, fatty, or starchy foods; rather, offer leftover meats, vegetables, and gravies. Get in the habit of feeding your puppy or your grown dog his *own* daily meals of dog food. If ever you are in doubt about what foods and how much to serve, consult your veterinarian.

Four Paws Good 'N Plenty Feeder is designed to hold approximately 2 pounds of food. The Good 'N Plenty Waterer holds a generous 3 quarts. Both are designed for easy dismantling and cleaning.

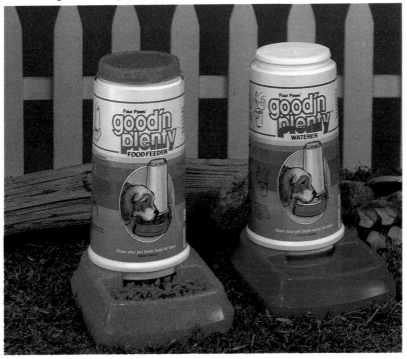

FEEDING GUIDELINES

Some things to bear in mind with regard to your dog's feeding regimen follow.

• Nutritional balance, provided by many commercial dog foods, is vital; avoid feeding a one-sided all-meat diet. Variety in the kinds of meat (beef, lamb, chicken, liver) or cereal grains (wheat, oats, corn) that you offer your dog is of secondary importance compared to the balance or "completeness" of dietary components.

• Always refrigerate opened canned food so that it doesn't spoil. Remember to remove all uneaten portions of canned or moistened food from the feeding dish as soon as the pup has finished his meal. Discard the leftover food immediately and thoroughly wash and dry the feeding dish, as a dirty dish is a breeding ground for harmful germs.

• When offering dry foods, always keep a supply of water on hand for your dog. Water should be made available at all times, even if dry foods are not left out for self-feeding. Each

Feeding your dog is made easy by the use of sturdy non-tip, easy-clean bowls. Pet shops offer the best selection of colors, styles and sizes.

day the water dish should be washed with soap and hot water, rinsed well, and dried; a refill of clean, fresh water should be provided daily.

• Food and water should be served at room temperature, neither too hot nor too cold, so that it is more palatable for your puppy.

• Serve your pup's meals in sturdy hard-plastic, stainless steel, or earthenware containers, ones that won't tip over as the dog gulps his food down. Some bowls and dishes are weighted to prevent spillage, while others fit neatly into holders which offer support. Feeding dishes should be large enough to hold each meal.

sessions.

• Hard foods, such as biscuits and dog meal, should be offered regularly. Chewing on these hard, dry morsels helps the dog keep its teeth clean and its gums conditioned.

• Never overfeed your dog. If given the chance, he will accept

New treats on the block by Nylabone®. These Chooz® crunchy dog bones are delectable and affordable.

• Whenever the nutritional needs of your dog change—that is to say, when it grows older or if it becomes ill, obese, or pregnant; or if it starts to nurse its young—special diets are in order. Always contact your vet for advice on these special dietary requirements.

• Feed your puppy at the same regular intervals each day; reserve treats for special occasions or, perhaps, to reward good behavior during training

and relish every in-between-meal tidbit you offer him. This pampering will only put extra weight on your pet and cause him to be unhealthy in the long run.

• Do not encourage your dog to beg for food from the table while you are eating your meals.

• Food can be effectively used by the owner to train the dog. Doggie treats are practical and often nutritional—choose your chew treats choosily.

FEEDING CHART

Age and No. of Feedings Per Day	Weight in Lbs.	Weight in Kg.	Caloric Requirement kcal M.E./Day
Puppies—Weaning to 3 months Four per day	1–3	.5–1.4	124–334
	3–6	1.4–2.7	334–574
	6–12	2.7–5.4	574–943
	12–20	5.4–9.1	943–1384
	15–30	6.8–13.6	1113–1872
Puppies—3 to 6 months Three per day	3–10	1.4–4.5	334–816
	5–15	2.3–6.8	494–1113
	12–25	5.4–11.3	943–1645
	20–40	9.1–18.2	1384–2352
	30–70	13.6–31.8	1872–3542
Puppies—6 to 12 months Two per day	6–12	2.7–5.4	574–943
	12–25	5.4–11.3	943–1645
	20–50	9.1–22.7	1384–2750
	40–70	18.2–31.8	2352–3542
	70–100	31.8–45.4	3542–4640
Normally Active Adults One or two per day	6–12	2.7–5.4	286–472
	12–25	5.4–11.3	472–823
	25–50	11.3–22.7	823–1375
	50–90	22.7–40.8	1375–2151
	90–175	40.8–79.4	2151–3675

This chart presents general parameters of the dog's caloric requirements, based on weight. The total caloric intake comes from a complete, balanced diet of quality foods. To assist owners, dog food companies generally provide the nutritional information to their product right on the label.

Accommodations

Puppies newly weaned from their mother and siblings should be kept warm at all times: As they get older, they can be acclimated gradually to cooler temperatures. When you purchase your dog, find out from the seller whether he is hardy and can withstand the rigors of outdoor living. Many breeds have been known to adapt well to a surprising number of environments, so long as they are given time to adjust. If your pup is to be an indoor companion, perhaps a dog bed in the corner of the family room will suffice; or you may want to invest in a crate for him to call his "home" whenever he needs to be confined for short intervals. You might plan to partition off a special room, or part of a room, for your pooch; or you may find that a heated garage or finished basement works well as your dog's living quarters. If your breed can tolerate living outside, you may want to buy or build him his own dog house with an attached run. It might be feasible to place his house in your fenced-in backyard. The breed that can live outdoors fares well when given access to some sort of warm, dry shelter during periods of inclement weather. As you begin thinking about where your canine friend will spend most of his time, you'll want to consider his breed, his age, his temperament, his need for exercise, and the money, space, and resources you have available to house him.

A bed for your dog gives him a place to call his own. His bed should be placed in a warm, dry, draft-free area.

THE DOG BED

In preparing for your puppy's arrival, it is recommended that a dog bed be waiting for him so that he has a place to sleep and rest. If you have provided him with his own bed or basket, ensure that it is placed in a warm, dry, draft-free spot that is private but at the same time near the center of family activity. Refrain from placing his bed near the feed and water dishes or his toilet area. You may want to give your puppy something with which to snuggle, such as a laundered towel or blanket or an article of old clothing. Some dogs have been known to chew apart their beds and bedding, but you can easily channel this chewing energy into more constructive

behavior simply by supplying him with some safe toys or a Nylabone® pacifier for gnawing. Pet shops stock dog beds, among other supplies that you might need for your pup. Select a bed that is roomy, comfortable, and easy to clean, keeping in mind that you may have to replace the smaller bed with a larger one as the puppy grows to adulthood. Remember to clean and disinfect the bed and sleeping area from time to time, as these can become parasitic playgrounds for fleas, lice, mites, and the like.

Beds can have personality. Pet shops offer many different bedding options to the owner willing to explore.

The wire crate is a most effective means to accelerate housebreaking and is the safest way to ensure that the puppy is safe when he cannot be supervised.

THE CRATE

Although many dog lovers may cringe at the mere mention of the word *crate,* thinking of it as a cage or a cruel means of confinement, this handy piece of equipment can be put to good use for puppies and grown dogs alike. Even though you may love your dog to an extraordinary degree, you may not want him to have free reign of the house, particularly when you are not home to supervise him. If used properly, a crate can restrict your dog when it is not convenient to have him underfoot, *i.e.,* when guests are visiting or during your mealtimes.

A surprising number of dog owners, who originally had negative feelings about crating their dogs, have had great success using crates. The crate itself serves as a bed, provided it is furnished with bedding material, or it can be used as an indoor dog house. Not all dogs readily accept crates or being confined in them for short

Four Paws offers a wide range of shampoos for every need: from flea and tick to medicated and many others. All shampoos are pH balanced for a gentle yet effective cleaning.

intervals, so for these dogs, another means of restriction must be found. But for those dogs that do adjust to spending time in these structures, the crate can be useful in many ways. The animal can be confined for a few hours while you are away from home or at work, or you can bring your crated dog along with you in the car when you travel or go on vacation. Crates also prove handy as carriers whenever you have to transport a sick dog to the veterinarian.

Most crates are made of sturdy wire or plastic, and some of the collapsible models can be conveniently stored or folded so that they can be moved easily from room to room or from inside the house to the yard on a warm, sunny day. If you allow your puppy or grown dog to become acquainted with its crate by cleverly propping the door open and leaving some of his favorite toys inside, in no time he will come to regard the crate as his own doggie haven. As with a dog bed, place the crate away from drafts in a dry, warm spot; refrain from placing food and water dishes in it, as these only crowd the space and offer opportunity for spillage.

If you need to confine your puppy so that he can't get into mischief while you're not home, remember to consider the animal's needs at all times. Select a large crate, one in which the dog can stand up and move around comfortably; in fact, bigger is better in this context. Never leave the animal confined for more than a few hours at a time without letting him out to exercise, play, and, if necessary, relieve himself. Never crate a dog for ten hours, for example, unless you keep the door to the crate open so that he can get out for food and water and to stretch a bit. If long intervals of confinement are necessary, consider placing the unlatched crate in a partitioned section of your house or apartment.

Crates have become the answer for many a dog owner faced with the dilemma of either getting rid of a destructive dog or living with him despite his bad habits. People who have neither the time nor the patience to train their dogs, or to modify undesirable behavior patterns, can at least restrain their pets during the times they can't be there to supervise. So long as the crate is used in a humane fashion, whereby a dog is

Traveling crates can provide safe and easy transport for your dog. Ventilation for travel is a most important consideration.

confined for no more than a few hours at any one time, it can figure importantly in a dog owner's life. Show dogs, incidentally, learn at an early age that much time will be spent in and out of crates while they are on the show circuit. Many canine celebrities are kept in their crates until they are called to ringside, and they spend many hours crated to and from the shows.

THE DOG HOUSE

These structures, often made of wood, should be sturdy and offer enough room for your dog to stretch out in when it rests or sleeps. Dog houses that are elevated or situated on a platform protect the animal from cold and dampness that may seep through the ground. For the breeds that are temperature hardy and will live outdoors, a dog house is an excellent option for daytime occupancy. Owners who cannot provide indoor accommodations for their chosen dog should consider a smaller breed since no dog should lead an exclusively outdoor existence.

If you have no option but to accommodate your dog with only an outdoor house, it will be necessary to provide him with a more elaborate house, one that really protects him from the elements. Make sure the dog's house is constructed of waterproof materials. Furnish

The pet trade offers many commercially made dog houses and other outdoor living structures that make great temporary accommodations for your pet.

Indoor-outdoor dog houses offer pest-free, sanitary conditions for your dog. These attractive living options can be acquired from pet shops or supply outlets.

him with sufficient bedding to burrow into on a chilly night and provide extra insulation to keep out drafts and wet weather. Add a partition (a kind of room divider which separates the entry area from the main sleeping space) inside his house or attach a swinging door to the entrance to help keep him warm when he is inside his residence. The swinging door facilitates entry to and from the dog house, while at the same time it provides protection, particularly from wind and drafts.

Some fortunate owners whose yards are enclosed by high fencing allow their dogs complete freedom within the boundaries of their property. In these situations, a dog can leave his dog house and get all the exercise he wants. Of course such a large space requires more effort to keep it clean. An alternative to complete backyard freedom is a dog kennel or run which attaches to or surrounds the dog's house. This restricts some forms of movement, such as running, perhaps, but it does provide ample room for walking, climbing, jumping, and stretching. Another option is to fence off part of the yard and place the dog house in the enclosure. If you need to tether your dog to its house, make certain to use a fairly long lead so as not to hamper the animal's need to move and exercise his limbs.

An anchored lead can provide efficient temporary restraint. This is not a viable substitute for a fenced-in yard and no dog should be left unsupervised on such a lead for any length of time.

CLEANLINESS

No matter where your dog lives, either in or out of your home, be sure to keep him in surroundings that are as clean and sanitary as possible. His excrement should be removed and disposed of every day without fail. No dog should be forced to lie in his own feces. If your dog lives in his own house, the floor should be swept occasionally and the bedding should be changed regularly if it becomes soiled. Food and water dishes need to be scrubbed with hot water and detergent and rinsed well to remove all traces of soap. The water dish should be refilled with a supply of fresh water. The dog and his environment must be kept free of parasites (especially fleas and mosquitoes, which can carry disease) with products designed to keep these pests under control. Dog crates need frequent scrubbing, too, as do the floors of kennels and runs. Your pet must be kept clean and comfortable at all times; if you exercise strict sanitary control, you will keep disease and parasite infestation to a minimum.

EXERCISE

A well-balanced diet and regular medical attention from a qualified veterinarian are essential in promoting good health for your dog, but so is daily exercise to keep him fit and mentally alert. Dogs that have been confined all day while their owners are at work or school need special attention. There should be some time set aside each day for play—a romp with a family member, perhaps. Not everyone is lucky enough to let his dog run through an open meadow or along a sandy beach, but even a ten-minute walk in the fresh air will do. Dogs that are house-bound, particularly those that live in apartments, need to be walked out-of-doors after each meal so that they can relieve themselves. Owners can make this daily ritual more pleasant both for themselves and their canine companions by combining the walk with a little "roughhousing," that is to say, a bit of fun and togetherness.

Whenever possible, take a stroll to an empty lot, a playground, or a nearby park. Attach a long lead to your dog's collar, and let him run and jump and tone his body through aerobic activity. This will help him burn calories and will keep him trim, and it will also help relieve tension and stress that may have had a chance to develop while you were away all day. For people who work Monday through Friday,

weekend jaunts can be especially beneficial, since there will be more time to spend with your canine friend. You might want to engage him in a simple game of fetch with a stick or a rubber ball. Even such basic tricks as rolling over, standing on the hindlegs, or jumping up (all of which can be done inside

Four Paws Stain & Odor Remover contains active enzymes to remove tough urine stains and the odor that attracts puppies to the previously soiled area.

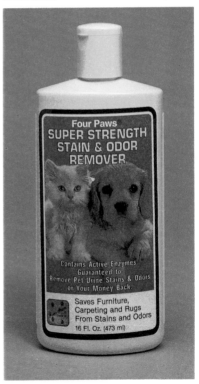

the home as well) can provide additional exercise. But if you plan to challenge your dog with a real workout to raise his heart rate, remember not to push him too hard without first warming up with a brisk walk. Don't forget to "cool him down" afterwards with a rhythmic trot until his heart rate returns to normal. Some dog owners jog with their dogs or take them along on bicycle excursions.

At the very least, however, play with your dog every day to keep him in good shape physically and mentally. If you can walk him outdoors, or better

yet run with him in a more vigorous activity, by all means do it. Don't neglect your pet and leave him confined for long periods without attention from you or time for exercise.

EXERCISING FOR YOU AND YOUR DOG

Dogs are like people. They come in three weights: overweight, underweight, and the correct weight. It is fair to say that most dogs are in better shape than most humans who own them. The reason for this is that most dogs accept exercise without objection—

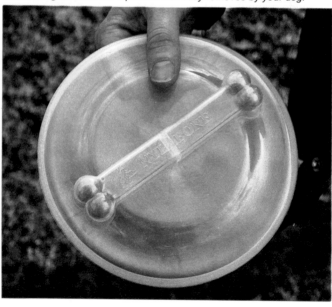

The most popular in flying discs designed especially for dogs is the Nylabone Frisbee®, a toy that outlasts plastic discs by ten times. The molded dog bone on the top makes for easy retrieves by your dog.

people do not! Follow your dog's lead towards exercise and the complete enjoyment of the outdoors—your dog is the ideal work-out partner. There are toys at your local pet shop which are designed just for that purpose: to allow you to play and exercise with your dog. Here are a few recommended exercise toys for you and your dog.

Frisbee® Flying Discs® Most dog owners capitalize on the dog's natural instinct to fetch or retrieve, and the Frisbee® flying disc is standard fare for play. The original Frisbee® is composed of polyethylene plastic, ideal for flying and great for games of catch between two humans. Since humans don't usually chew on their flying discs, there is no need for a "chew-worthy" construction material. Dogs, on the other hand, do chew on their Frisbees® and therefore should not be allowed to play with a standard original Frisbee®. These discs will be destroyed quickly by the dog and the rigid plastic can cause intestinal complications.

Nylon Discs More suitable for playing with dogs are the Frisbee® discs that are constructed from nylon. These durable Frisbee® discs are designed especially for dogs and the nearly indestructible

manufacturing makes them ideal for aggressive chewing dogs. For play with dogs, the nylon discs called Nylabone Frisbee® are guaranteed to last ten times as long as the regular plastic Frisbee®. Owners should

Made of durable and flexible polyurethane, the Gumabone® Frisbees® prove chew-worthy and good-smelling to dogs. These and other Nylabone® discs are available in pet shops and other stores.

carefully consider the size of the nylon Frisbee® they purchase. A rule of thumb is choose the largest disc that your dog can comfortably carry. Nylabone manufactures two

Dogs enjoy toys they can carry around. The Gumaring® is a favorite plaything for many dogs.

The Tug Toy from Gumabone® is a flavorable exercise device that can be enjoyed by dog and owner.

sizes only—toy and large—so the choice should be apparent.

Polyurethane Flexible Floppy Flying Discs The greatest advance in flying discs came with the manufacture of these discs from polyurethane. The polyurethane is so soft that it doesn't hurt you, your dog, or the window it might strike accidentally. The polyurethane Gumadisc® is floppy and soft. It can be folded and fits into your pocket. It is also much tougher than cheap plastics, and most pet shops guarantee that it will last ten times longer than cheap plastic discs.

Making the polyurethane discs even more suited to dog play is the fact that many of the Gumabone® Frisbee® Flexible Fly Discs have the advantage of a dog bone molded on the top. Very often a Frisbee® without the bone molded on the top is difficult for a dog to pick up when it lands on a flat surface. The molded ones enable the dog to grasp it with his mouth or turn it with his paw. Dogs love pawing at the bone and even chew on it occasionally.

This product has one further capacity—it doubles

as a temporary drinking dish while out running, hiking and playing. The Gumabone Frisbee® flyers may also be flavored or scented, besides being annealed, so your dog can find it more easily if it should get lost in woods or tall grass.

Flying discs manufactured by the Nylabone® Company may cost more than some of its imitators, but an owner can be assured that the product will last and not be quickly destroyed.

With most flying discs made for dogs comes an instruction booklet on how to use the disc with your canine friend. Basically, you play with the dog and the disc so the dog knows the disc belongs to him. Then you throw it continuously, increasing the distance, so that the dog fetches it and brings it back to you.

The exercise for you comes in when your dog stops fetching it, or when you have a partner. The two of you play catch. You stand as far apart as available space allows—usually 30–35 m

(100 feet) is more than enough room. You throw the disc to each other, arousing your dog's interest as he tries to catch it.

Dental floss devices from Nylabone® serve two excellent purposes: good exercise and clean teeth.

When the disc is dropped or veers off, the dog grabs it and brings it back (hopefully). Obviously you will have to run to catch the disc before your dog does.

There are contests held all over the world where distance, height, and other characteristics are measured competitively. Ask your local pet shop to help you locate a Frisbee® Club near you.

*Frisbee® is a trademark of the Kransco Company, California, and is used for their brand of flying disc.

Tug Toys A tug toy is a hard rubber, cheap plastic, or polyurethane toy which allows a dog and his owner to have a game of tug-o-war. The owner grips one end while the dog grips the other—then they pull. The polyurethane flexible tug toy is the best on the market at the present time. Your pet shop will have one to show you. The polyurethane toys are clear in color and stay soft forever. Cheap plastic tug toys are indisputably dangerous, and the hard-rubber tug toys get brittle too fast and are too stiff for most dogs; however, there *is* a difference in price—just ask the advice of any pet shop operator.

It pays to invest in entertainment toys and exercise devices which are marketed particularly for dogs. These products outlast everyday play things and are much safer for your pet. The Gumaball® is a great example of a dog toy worth the price of admission.

Balls Nobody has to tell you about playing ball with your dog. The reminder you may need is that you should not throw the ball where traffic might interfere with the dog's catching or fetching of it. The ball should not be cheap plastic (a dog's worst enemy as far as toys are concerned) but made of a substantial material. Balls made of nylon are practically indestructible, but they are very hard and must be rolled, never thrown. The same balls made of polyurethane are great—they bounce and are soft. The Nylaballs® and Gumaballs® are scented and flavored, and dogs can easily find them when lost.

Other manufacturers make balls of almost every substance, including plastic, cotton, and wood. Soft balls, baseballs, tennis balls, and so on, have all been used by dog owners who want their dogs to play with them in a game of catch. A strong caveat is that you use only those balls made especially for dogs.

Preventive Dental Care

ALL DOGS NEED TO CHEW

Puppies and young dogs need something with resistance to chew on while their teeth and jaws are developing—to cut the puppy teeth, to induce growth of the permanent teeth under the puppy teeth, to assist in getting rid of the puppy teeth on time, to help the permanent teeth through the gums, to assure

An artist's representation of the calculus index, ranging from index rating 4 (topmost drawing) through index rating 1 (lowest drawing).

4 *Buccal crown covered*
3 *⅔ crown covered*
2 *⅓ crown covered*
1 *Only gingival margin covered*
0 *No calculus evident*

normal jaw development and to settle the permanent teeth solidly in the jaws.

The adult dog's desire to chew stems from the instinct for tooth cleaning, gum massage, and jaw exercise—plus the need to vent periodic doggie tensions. . . . A pacifier if you will!

Dental caries, as they affect the teeth of humans, are virtually unknown in dogs; but tartar (calculus) accumulates on the teeth of dogs, particularly at the gum line, more rapidly than on the teeth of humans. These accumulations, if not removed, bring irritation and then infection, which erode the tooth enamel and ultimately destroy the teeth at the roots. It is important that you take your dog to your local veterinarian for periodic dental examinations.

Tooth and jaw development will normally continue until the dog is more than a year old—but sometimes much longer, depending upon the dog, its chewing exercise, rate of calcium utilization and many other factors, known and unknown, which affect the development of individual dogs. Diseases, like distemper for example, may sometimes arrest development of the teeth and jaws, which may resume months or even years later.

This is why dogs, especially puppies and young dogs, will

often destroy valuable property when their chewing instinct is not diverted from their owners' possessions, particularly during the widely varying critical period for young dogs. Saving your possessions from destruction, assuring proper development of teeth and jaws, providing for "interim" tooth cleaning and gum massage, and channeling doggie tensions into a non-destructive outlet are, therefore, all dependent upon the dog's having something suitable for chewing readily available when his instinct tells him to chew. If your purposes, and those of your dog, are to be accomplished, what you provide for chewing must be desirable from the doggie viewpoint, have the necessary functional qualities, and, above all, be safe.

It is very important that dogs be prohibited from chewing on anything they can break or indigestible things from which they can bite sizeable chunks. Sharp pieces, such as those from a bone which can be broken by a dog, may pierce the intestinal wall and kill. Indigestible things which can be bitten off in chunks, such as toys made of rubber compound or cheap plastic, may cause an intestinal stoppage; if not regurgitated, they are certain to bring painful death unless surgery is promptly performed.

NATURAL CHEW BONES

Strong natural bones, such as 4- to 8-inch lengths of round shin bone from mature beef—either the kind you can get from your butcher or one of the varieties available commercially in pet stores—may serve your dog's teething needs, if his mouth is large enough to handle them effectively, *but,* constant chewing on hard bones wears down a dog's teeth. Natural bones are very abrasive and should be used sparingly.

You may be tempted to give your puppy a smaller bone and he may not be able to break it when you do, but puppies grow rapidly and the power of their jaws constantly increases until maturity. This means that a growing dog may break one of the smaller bones at any time, swallow the pieces and die painfully before you realize what is wrong.

Many people have the mistaken notion that their dog's teeth are like those of wild carnivores or of dogs from antiquity. The teeth of wild carnivorous animals and those found in the fossils of the dog-like creatures of antiquity have far thicker and stronger enamel than those of our dogs today.

All hard natural bones are highly abrasive. If your dog is an avid chewer, natural bones may wear away his teeth

Rawhide treats are enjoyed by dogs. Owners should be wary since rawhide can tear off in large pieces and lodge in the dog's throat or cause intestinal blockage.

prematurely; hence, they then should be taken away from your dog when the teething purposes have been served. The badly worn, and usually painful, teeth of many mature dogs can be traced to excessive chewing on animal bones. Contrary to popular belief, knuckle bones that can be chewed up and swallowed by the dog provide little, if any, useable calcium or other nutrient. They do, however, disturb the digestion of most dogs and might cause them to vomit the nourishing food they really need.

Never give a dog your old shoe to chew on, even if you have removed all the nails or metal parts, such as lace grommets, buckles, metal arches, and so on. Rubber heels are especially dangerous, as the dog can bite off chunks, swallow them, and suffer from intestinal blockage as a result.

Additionally, if the rubber should happen to have a nail imbedded in it that you cannot detect, this could pierce or tear the intestinal wall. There is always the possibility, too, that your dog may fail to differentiate between his shoe and yours and chew up a good pair while you're not looking. It is strongly recommended that you refrain from offering old shoes as chew toys, since there are much safer products available.

Rawhide treats are popular choices for dogs. Owners are advised to keep an eye on their dogs whenever they are playing with rawhide.

RAWHIDE CHEWS

The most popular material from which dog chews are made is the hide from cows, horses, and other animals. Most of these chews are made in foreign countries where the quality of the hide is not good enough for making leather. These foreign hides may contain lead, antibiotics, arsenic, or insecticides which might be detrimental to the health of your dog…or even your children. It is not impossible that a small child will start chewing on a piece of rawhide meant for the dog! Rawhide chews do not serve the primary chewing functions very well. They are also a bit messy when wet from mouthing, and most dogs chew them up rather rapidly. They have been considered safe for dogs until recently.

Rawhide is flavorful to dogs. They like it. Currently, some veterinarians have been attributing cases of acute constipation to large pieces of incompletely digested rawhide in the intestine. Basically it is good for them to chew on, but dogs think rawhide is food. They do not play with it nor do they use it as a pacifier to relieve doggie tension. They eat it as they would any other food. This is dangerous, for the hide is very difficult for dogs to digest and swallow, and many dogs choke on large particles of rawhide that become stuck in their throats. *Before you offer your dog rawhide chews, consult your veterinarian.* Vets have a lot of experience with canine chewing devices; ask them what they recommend.

NYLON CHEW DEVICES

The nylon bones, especially those with natural meat and bone flavor added, are probably the most complete, safe, and economical answer to the chewing need. Dogs cannot break them nor bite off sizeable chunks; hence, they are completely safe. And being longer lasting than other things offered for the purpose, they are very economical.

Hard chewing raises little bristle-like projections on the surface of the nylon bones to provide effective interim tooth cleaning and vigorous gum massage, much in the same way your toothbrush does it for you. The little projections are raked off and swallowed in the form of thin shavings, but the chemistry of the nylon is such that they break down in the stomach fluids and pass through without effect.

The toughness of the nylon provides the strong chewing resistance needed for important jaw exercise and effective help for the teething functions; however, there is no tooth wear because nylon is non-abrasive. Being inert, nylon does not

Annealed nylon and polyurethane chew toys are recommended by veterinarians as proven-safe and effective canine chew devices.

Polyurethane bones come in many colors and sizes. The Rainbows collection from Gumabone® adds flair to any dog's dental hygiene program.

support the growth of microorganisms, and it can be washed in soap and water or sterilized by boiling or in an autoclave.

There are a great variety of Nylabone® products available that veterinarians recommend as safe and healthy for your dog or puppy to chew on. These Nylabone® Pooch Pacifiers® usually don't splinter, chip, or break off in large chunks; instead, they are frizzled by the dog's chewing action, and this creates a toothbrush-like surface that cleanses the teeth and massages the gums. At the

same time, these hard-nylon therapeutic devices channel doggie tension and chewing frustation into constructive rather than destructive behavior. The original nylon bone (Nylabone®) is not a toy and dogs use it only when in need of pacification. Keeping a bone in each of your dog's recreation rooms is the best method of providing the requisite pacification. Unfortunately, many nylon chew products have been copied. These inferior quality copies are sold in supermarkets and other chain stores. The really good products are sold only through veterinarians, pet shops, grooming salons and places where the sales people really know something about dogs. The good products have the flavor impregnated *into* the bone. This makes the taste last longer. The smell is undetectable to humans. The artificial bones which have a strong odor are poor-quality bones with the odor sprayed on to impress the dog owner (not the dog)! These heavily scented dog toys may impart the odor to your carpets or furniture if an odor-sprayed bone lies there wet from a dog's chewing on it.

FLOSS OR LOSS!

Most dentists relay that brushing daily is just not enough. In order to prevent unnecessary tooth loss, flossing is essential. For dogs, human dental floss is not the answer—however, canine dental devices are available. The Nylafloss® is a revolutionary product that is designed to save dogs teeth and keep them healthy. Even though your dogs won't believe you, Nylafloss® is not a toy but rather a most effective agent in removing destructive plaque between the teeth and *beneath* the gum line where gum disease begins. Gentle tugging is all that is necessary to activate the Nylafloss®. These 100% inert nylon products are guaranteed

to outlast rawhide chews by ten times and are available for sale at all pet shops.

THE IMPORTANCE OF PREVENTION

In order to get to the root of canine dentistry problems, it is important for owners to realize that no less than 75% of all canine dental health problems, serious enough to require a vet's assistance, and nearly 98% of all canine teeth lost are attributable to periodontal disease. Periodontal disease not only mars the teeth but also the gums and other buccal tissue in the mouth. Severe cases of periodontal disease involve resultant bacterial toxins which are absorbed into the blood

The Nylafloss® cannot cure tooth decay, but it is an optimum decay-prevention device. Make your dog's playtime a healthy time and invest in your pet's future.

stream and cause permanent damage to the heart and kidneys. In the infected mouth, teeth are loosened; tartar, unsightly and bad smelling, accumulates heavily; and the dog experiences a complete

The moderate calculus build-up on this dog's teeth reflects a certain neglect by the owner. Providing a safe chew item like the Gumabone® can help save your dog's teeth.

loss of appetite. Long-standing periodontitis can also manifest itself in simple symptoms such as diarrhea and vomiting.

Periodontal disease deserves the attention of every dog owner—a dog's teeth are extremely important to his ongoing health. The accumulation of plaque, food matter mixed with saliva attaching itself to the tooth surface, is a sure sign of potential bacteria build-up. As

toxic material gathers, the bone surrounding the teeth erodes. If plaque and calculus continue to reside without attention, bacteria-fighting cells will form residual pus at the root of the teeth, dividing the gum from the tooth. The debris is toxic and actually kills the buccal tissue. This is a most undesirable situation, as hardened dental calculus is one of the most direct causative agents of periodontitis.

In actuality, the disease is a result of a number of contributing factors. Old age, a diet comprised solely of soft or semi-soft foods, dental tartar, constant chewing of hair and even coprophagy (the eating of stool) are among the most common contributors.

Just as regular dental visits and brushing are necessary for humans, regular hygienic care and veterinary check-ups can help control tooth problems in canines. Involved and expensive routines can be performed on the affected, neglected mouth and teeth if decay has begun eroding the enamel and infecting the gums. Cleaning, polishing, and scaling are routine to remove calculus build-up.

Owners must claim responsibility for their dog's health, and tooth care is no small aspect of the care required. Daily brushing with a salt/baking soda solution is the best answer, but many owners find this tedious or just too difficult to perform. The simpler and more proven effective way to avoid, reduce, and fight periodontal disease and calculus build-up is giving the dog regular access to a thermoplastic polymer chew device. The Gumabone® products are the only scientifically proven line that offers the desired protection from calculus and tartar build-up.

Regular use of the Gumabone® chew products can significantly reduce plaque build-up.

CANINE DENTAL BREAKTHROUGH

The independent research of Dr. Andrew Duke, D.V.M., reveals that 70% of the dogs that regularly use Gumabone® experience a reduction of calculus build-up. This find is a breakthrough for the dog world, since the Gumabone® has already resided in the toy boxes of many dogs as their favorite play item. Little did owners know previously that their dogs were gaining entertainment and unparalleled dental treatment at the same time. Dr. Duke writes: "There is little debate left that dental calculus is an excellent indicator of periodontal health in the dog, just as it is in humans. "Calculus does not cause gingivitis and periodontitis, but the plaque and bacteria that cause periodontitis are

responsible for the mineral precipitation we know as 'calculus.' All veterinarians who have made a study of dogs' oral health have noticed the middle aged dog who actively chews with excellent gingival health. Many of these dogs that chew

Teeth of an infected dog showing little to no plaque accumulation after professional cleaning.

hard substances regularly wear the cusps down and even may expose the pulp cavity faster than secondary dentin can be formed. Often these "excellent chewers" are presented with slab fractures of the premolars or apical abcesses.

"The challenge then becomes to find a substance which is effective in removing calculus and plaque but does not wear the enamel excessively. In an attempt to duplicate the chewstuffs enjoyed by dogs in the wild, researchers have used bovine tracheas to demonstrate the inhibition of plaque and gingivitis. Very little else has been done in veterinary medicine to establish a scientific basis for evaluating chewstuffs.

"In the human field it is generally accepted (incorrectly) that fibrous foodstuffs and diet have no effect on oral health. This is a moot point since the practice of brushing is by far a more efficient technique of preventing plaque accumulation, calculus and periodontal disease. Studies in human subjects failed to find any benefits in eating apples, raw carrots, etc. If people are not allowed to brush, it is difficult to

The clean healthy teeth that are desired in dogs should inspire owners to work towards better dental hygiene.

Plaque is formed by the food debris and bacterial deposits left on teeth. Due to the high carbon dioxide and pH levels in the mouth, minerals precipitate quickly on the plaque to form calculus.

conduct clinical trials of more than one week.

"The increased awareness of animals' dental health of recent years has resulted in most veterinary practitioners' recommending some kind of chewstuff to their dog owners. To meet this market demand, there has been a stampede into the market by vendors ready to promote their products. The veterinarian is furnished no scientific data, but is asked to promote rawhide, bounce, and squeaky toys. How would our human colleagues handle this situation? Can Listerine® say that it prevents colds, but not support the claim? Can "Tartar Control Crest®" or "Colgate Tartar Control Formula®" be sold if it is not proven that it does in fact reduce tartar? Of course not.

"To this end, the following study was made.

"*Method:* Twenty dogs of different breeds and age were selected from a veterinary

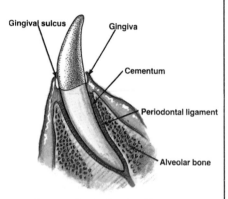

Gingival sulcus
Gingiva
Cementum
Periodontal ligament
Alveolar bone

Comparative look at healthy gums (above) and affected gums (below) in a dog's mouth. Instinctively dogs need to massage their gums—and the Gumabone® can satisfy this doggie craving.

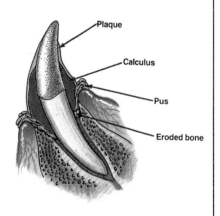

Plaque
Calculus
Pus
Eroded bone

practice's clientele. Although most were from multiple pet households, none were colony dogs. The owners were asked if they would allow their dogs to be anesthetized for two prophylactic cleanings which included root planing, polishing, and gingival debridement necessary to insure good oral hygiene.

"The dogs were divided into two groups of 10. Their teeth were cleaned and their calculus index converted to 0. One group was allowed only their normal dry commercial dog ration for 30 days. The other was allowed to have free choice access to Gumabone® products of the appropriate size.

"After 30 days, photoslides were made of the upper 3rd premolar, upper 4th premolar, and the lower 4th premolar on both sides of the dog's mouth. The dogs were again subjected to a prophylactic cleaning and the group reversed. After the second 30 days, photoslides were again made. A total of six teeth in each mouth were evaluated on each dog. This was 80 slides representing 240 teeth."

Fourteen out of 20 dogs (or 70%) experienced a reduction in calculus build-up by regularly using the Gumabone® product. These products are available in a variety of sizes (for different

Nylabone® and Gumabone® offer a new option for the choosy canine–chicken-flavored bones. Entertainment and pearly white teeth have never been better acquainted.

size dogs) and designed in interesting shapes: bones, balls, knots and rings (and even a tug toy). The entertainment value of the Gumabone® products is but an added advantage to the fighting of tooth decay and periodontitis. The products are ham-flavored and made of a thermoplastic polymer that is designed to outlast by ten times any rawhide, rubber or vinyl chew product, none of which can promise the proven benefit of the Gumabone®.

If your dog is able to chew apart a Gumabone®, it is probable that you provided him with a bone that is too small for him. Replace it with a larger one and the problem should not re-materialize. Economically, the Gumabone® is a smart choice, even without comparing it to the cost of extensive dental care.

Of course, nothing can *substitute* for periodic

In cases of bad neglect, scaling a dog's teeth can help to save or salvage affected teeth. Your veterinarian can perform this procedure.

professional attention to your dog's teeth and gums, no more than your toothbrush can replace your dentist. Have your dog's teeth cleaned by your veterinarian at least once a year—twice a year is better—and he will be healthier, happier, and a far more pleasant companion.

Gumabones® are available through veterinarians and pet shops.

Canine tooth brushes are designed to allow access to the most hard-to-reach places in the canine mouth. Accustom your dog to brushing from puppyhood.

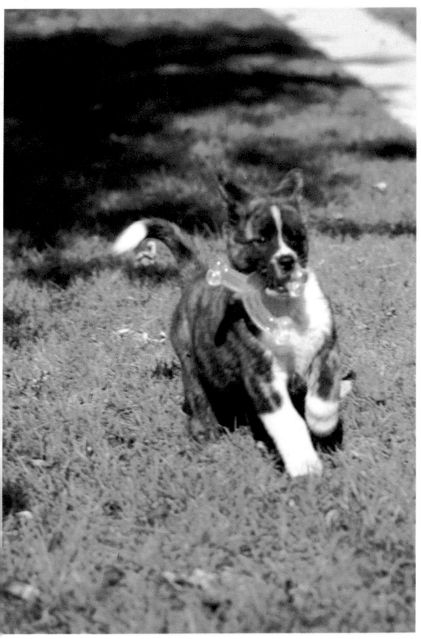

Exercise, fun and good dental hygiene go paw in paw. This energetic Akita pup is enjoying his Gumabone chew toy. Owner, Windom Akitas.

Housebreaking and Training

HOUSEBREAKING

The new addition to your family may already have received some basic house training before his arrival in your home. If he has not, remember that a puppy will want to relieve himself about half a dozen times a day; it is up to you to specify where and when he should "do his business." Housebreaking is your first training concern and should begin the moment you bring the puppy home.

Ideally, puppies should be taken outdoors after meals, as a full stomach will exert pressure on the bladder and colon. What goes into the dog must eventually come out; the period

Four Paws Wee-Wee Pads are scientifically treated to attract puppies when nature calls. The plastic lining prevents damage to floors and carpets.

after his meal is the most natural and appropriate time. When he eliminates, he should be praised, for this will increase the likelihood of the same thing happening after every meal. He should also be encouraged to use the same area and will probably be attracted to it after frequent use.

Some veterinarians maintain that a puppy can learn to urinate and defecate on command, if properly trained. The advantage of this conditioning technique is that your pet will associate the act of elimination with a particular word of your choice rather than with a particular time or place which might not always be convenient or available. So whether you are visiting an unfamiliar place or don't want to go outside with your dog in sub-

zero temperatures, he will still be able to relieve himself when he hears the specific command word. Elimination will occur after this "trigger" phrase or word sets up a conditioned reflex in the dog, who will eliminate anything contained in his bladder or bowel upon hearing it. The shorter the word, the more you can repeat it and imprint it on your dog's memory.

Your chosen command word should be given simultaneously with the sphincter opening events in order to achieve perfect and rapid conditioning. This is why it is important to familiarize yourself with the tell-tale signs preceding your puppy's elimination process. Then you will be prepared to say the word at the crucial moment. There is usually a sense of

Crates assist in house-training the puppy. The dog's natural instinct is never to soil his sleeping area.

urgency on the dog's part; he may follow a sniffing and circling pattern which you will soon recognize. It is important to use the command in his usual area only when you know the puppy can eliminate, i.e., when his stomach or bladder is full. He will soon learn to associate the act with the word. One word of advice, however, if you plan to try out this method: never use the puppy's name or any other word which he might frequently hear about the house—you can imagine the result!

Finally, remember that any training takes time. Such a conditioned response can be obtained with intensive practice with any normal, healthy dog over six weeks of age. Even Pavlov's salivating dogs required fifty repetitions before the desired response was achieved. Patience and persistence will eventually produce results—do not lose heart!

Indoors, sheets of newspapers can be used to cover the specific area where your dog should relieve himself. These should be placed some distance away from his sleeping and feeding area, as a puppy

This future show dog is learning the ins and outs of the exhibition world. Visiting dog shows when the pup is young is a good way to foster his socialization to crowds and other dogs.

Show training or just general obedience training must be practiced at home. Akitas require training from the earliest age so that they will not be unmanageable and disobedient as young adults. Owner, Windom Akitas.

The choke collar and walking lead are commonly used in training.

will not urinate or defecate where he eats. When the newspapers are changed, the bottom papers should be placed on top of the new ones in order to reinforce the purpose of the papers by scent as well as by sight. The puppy should be praised during or immediately after he has made use of this particular part of the room. Each positive reinforcement increases the possibility of his using that area again.

When he arrives, it is advisable to limit the puppy to one room, usually the kitchen, as it most likely has a linoleum or easily washable floor surface. Given the run of the house, the sheer size of the place will seem overwhelming and confusing and he might leave his "signature" on your furniture or clothes! There will be time later to familiarize him gradually with his new surroundings.

PATIENCE, PERSISTENCE, AND PRAISE

As with a human baby, you must be patient, tolerant, and understanding of your pet's mistakes, making him feel loved and wanted, not rejected and isolated. You wouldn't hit a baby for soiling his diapers, as you would realize that he was not yet able to control his bowel movements; be as compassionate with your canine infant. Never rub his nose in his excreta. Never indulge in the common practice of punishing him with a rolled-up newspaper. Never hit a puppy with your hand. He will only become "hand-shy" and learn to fear you. Usually the punishment is meted out sometime after the offense and loses its efficacy, as the bewildered dog cannot connect the two events. Moreover, by association, he will soon learn to be afraid of you and anything to do with newspapers—including, perhaps, that area where he is

supposed to relieve himself!

Most puppies are eager to please. Praise, encouragement, and reward (particularly the food variety) will produce far better results than any scolding or physical punishment. Moreover, it is far better to dissuade your puppy from doing certain things, such as chewing on chair legs or other furniture, by making those objects particularly distasteful to him. Some pet shops stock bitter apple sprays or citronella compounds for application to furniture legs. These products are generally safer than old-fashioned home remedies. An owner may soon discover that application of these products may indeed make it seem as if

A simple dog collar or leash can be deceiving. Never be afraid to ask your pet shop proprietor exactly how a particular device is intended to work.

Temperament testing has become increasingly popular in the United States. In these tests, the dogs encounter strangers in strange circumstances and are expected to react in a certain way. Breeders must aim for consistency and evenness of temperament. There is never any excuse for an aggressive or unmanageable Akita.

the object itself was administering the punishment whenever he attempted to chew it. He probably wouldn't need a second reminder and your furniture will remain undamaged.

Remember that the reason a dog has housebreaking or behavior problems is because his owner has allowed them to develop. This is why you must begin as you intend to continue, letting your dog know what is acceptable and unacceptable behavior. It is also important that you be consistent in your demands; you cannot feed him from the dining room table one day and then punish him when he begs for food from your dinner guests.

TRAINING

You will want the newest member of your family to be welcomed by everyone; this will not happen if he urinates in every room of the house or barks all night! He needs training in the correct forms of behavior in this new human world. You cannot expect your puppy to become the perfect pet overnight. He needs your help in

This is Ako's Tomodaichi owned by Dr. Sanford Paul.

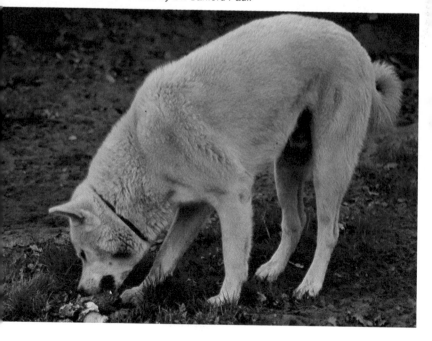

his socialization process. Training greatly facilitates and enhances the relationship of the dog to his owner and to the rest of society. A successfully trained dog can be taken anywhere and behave well with anyone. Indeed, it is that one crucial word—*training*—which can transform an aggressive animal into a peaceful, well-behaved pet. Now, how does this "transformation" take place?

WHEN AND HOW TO TRAIN

Like housebreaking, training should begin as soon as the puppy enters the house. The formal training sessions should be short but frequent, for example, ten to fifteen minute periods three times a day. These are much more effective than long, tiring sessions of half an hour which might soon become boring. You are building your relationship with your puppy during these times, so make them as enjoyable as possible. It is a good idea to have these sessions *before* the puppy's meal, not after it when he wouldn't feel like exerting himself; the dog will then associate something pleasurable with his training sessions and look forward to them.

A choke collar can be an effective training tool when properly used.

THE COLLAR AND LEASH

Your puppy should become used to a collar and leash as soon as possible. If he is very young, a thin, choke-chain collar can be used, but you will need a larger and heavier one for training when he is a little older. Remember to have his name and address on an identification tag attached to his collar, as you don't want to lose your pet if he should happen to leave your premises and explore the neighborhood!

Let the puppy wear his collar until he is used to how it feels. After a short time he will soon become accustomed to it and you can attach the leash. He might resist your attempts to lead him or simply sit down and refuse to budge. Fight him for a few minutes, tugging on the leash if necessary, then let him relax for the day. He won't be trained until he learns that he must obey the pull under any circumstance, but this will take a few sessions. Remember that a dog's period of concentration is short, so *little* and *often* is the wisest course of action—and patience is the password to success.

GIVING COMMANDS

When you begin giving your puppy simple commands, make them as short as possible and use the same word with the same meaning at all times, for example, "Heel," "Sit," and "Stay." You must be consistent; otherwise your puppy will become confused. The dog's name should prefix all commands to attract his attention. Do not become impatient with him however many times you have to repeat your command.

A good way to introduce the "Come" command is by calling the puppy when his meal is ready. Once this is learned, you can call your pet to you at will, always remembering to praise him for his prompt obedience. This "reward," or positive

Nylon and leather leads are the most popular with pet owners.

Providing young puppies with chew toys helps them understand what is acceptable to chew on and what is not. These Akita pups are playing with a Nylafloss dental device. Owner, Anthony DeMeo.

reinforcement, is such a crucial part of training that a Director of the New York Academy of Dog Training constructed his whole teaching program upon the methods of "Love, Praise, and Reward." Incidentally, if you use the command "Come," use it every time. Don't switch to "Come here" or "Come boy," as this will only confuse your dog.

Guaranteed by the manufacturer to stop any dog, any size, any weight from ever pulling again. It's like having power steering for your dog.

It is worth underlining the fact that punishment is an ineffective teaching technique. We have already seen this in housebreaking. For example, if your pup should run away, it would be senseless to beat him when he eventually returns; he would only connect the punishment with his return, not with running away! In addition, it is unwise to call him to you to punish him, as he will soon learn not to respond when you call his name.

SOME SPECIFIC COMMANDS

"**Sit**" This is one of the easiest and most useful commands for your dog to learn, so it is a good idea to begin with it. The only equipment required is a leash, a collar, and a few tasty tidbits. Take your dog out for some exercise before his meal. After about five minutes, call him to you, praise him when he arrives, and slip his collar on him. Hold the leash tightly in your right hand; this should force the dog's head up and focus his attention on you. As you say "Sit" in a loud, clear voice, with your left hand press steadily on his rump until he is in a sitting position. As soon as he is in the correct position, praise him and give him the tidbit you have in your hand. Now wait a few minutes to let him rest and repeat the routine. Through repetition, the dog soon associates the word with the act. Never make the lesson too long. Eventually your praise will be reward enough for your puppy. Other methods to teach this command exist, but this one, executed with care and moderation, has proven the most effective.

Great for the athletic dog and less-active owner are commercially designed retractable leads which give the dog much more freedom when exercising in an open field or cleared area.

"Sit-Stay/ Stay" To teach your pet to remain in one place or "stay" on your command, first of all order him to the sitting position at your side. Lower your left hand with the flat of your palm in front of his nose and your fingers pointing downwards. Hold the leash high and taut behind his head so that he cannot move. Speak the command "Sit-stay" and, as you are giving it, step in front of him. Repeat the command and tighten the leash so the animal cannot follow you. Walk completely around him, repeating the command and keeping him motionless by holding the leash at arm's length above him to check his movement. When he remains in this position for about fifteen seconds, you can begin the second part of the training. You will have to exchange the leash for a nylon cord or rope about twenty to thirty feet long. Repeat the whole routine from the beginning and be ready to prevent any movement towards you with a sharp "Sit-stay." Move around him in ever-widening circles until you are about fifteen feet away from him. If he still remains seated, you can pat yourself on the back! One useful thing to remember is that the dog makes associations with what you say, how you say it, and what you do while you are saying it. Give this command in a firm, clear tone of voice, perhaps using an admonishing forefinger raised, warning the dog to "stay."

"Heel" When you walk your dog, you should hold the leash firmly in your right hand. The dog should walk on your left so you have the leash crossing your body. This enables you to have greater control over the dog.

Let your dog lead you for the first few moments so that he fully understands that freedom can be his if he goes about it properly.

He already knows that when he wants to go outdoors the leash and collar are necessary, so he has respect for the leash. Now, if he starts to pull in one direction while walking, all you do is *stop walking*. He will walk a few steps and then find that he can't walk any further. He will then turn and look into your face. *This is the crucial point!* Just stand there for a moment and stare right back at him . . . now walk another ten feet and stop again. Again your dog will probably walk to the end of the leash, find he can't go any further, and turn around and look again. If he starts to pull and jerk, just stand there. After he quiets

Although your Akita pup is innocent and cute, without proper early training, he can grow up to be willful and disobedient.

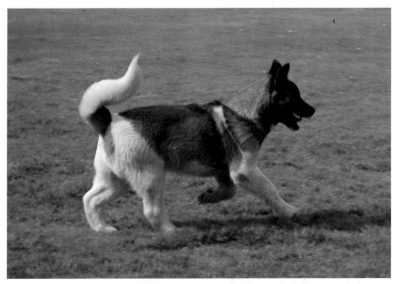

Never scold a dog for responding to your command. When a dog has responded to your come command, praise him with gusto. Handler, Fran Wasserman.

down, bend down and comfort him, as he may be frightened. Keep up this training until he learns not to outwalk you.

Once the puppy obeys the pull of the leash, half of your training is accomplished. "Heeling" is a necessity for a well-behaved dog, so teach him to walk beside you, head even with your knee. Nothing looks sadder than a big dog taking his helpless owner for a walk. It is annoying to passers-by and other dog owners to have a large dog, however friendly, bear down on them and entangle dogs, people, and packages.

To teach your dog, start off walking briskly, saying "Heel" in a firm voice. Pull back with a sharp jerk if he lunges ahead, and if he lags repeat the command and tug on the leash, not allowing him to drag behind. After the dog has learned to heel at various speeds on leash, you can remove it and practice heeling free, but have it ready to snap on again as soon as he wanders.

"Come" Your dog has already learned to come to you when you call his name. Why? Because you only call him when his food is ready or when you wish to play with him or praise him. Outdoors such a response is more difficult to achieve, if he is happily playing by himself or with other dogs, so he must be trained to come to you when he is called. To teach him to come, let him reach the end of a long lead, then give the command, gently pulling him towards you at the same time. As soon as he associates the word *come* with the action of moving towards you, pull only when he does not respond immediately. As he starts to come, move back to make him learn that he must come from a distance as well as when he is close to you. Soon you may be able to practice without a leash, but if he is slow to come or actively disobedient, go to him and pull him toward you, repeating the command. Always remember to reward his successful completion of a task.

"Down" Teaching the "down" command ideally begins while your dog is still a pup. During puppyhood your dog frequently will lie down, as this position is one of the dog's most natural positions. Invest some time, and keep close watch over your pup. Each time he begins to lie, repeat in a low convincing tone the word "down." If for the first day of training, you concur a majority of the dog's sitting with your commands and continue with reinforcement and moderate praise your pup should conquer the "down" command in no time.

Teaching the "down" command to a mature dog likely will require more effort. Although the lying position is still natural to a dog, his being forced into it is not. Some dogs may react with fear, anger, or confusion. Others may accept the process and prove quick learners. Have your dog sit and face you. If he is responsive and congenial, gently take his paws, and slowly pull them towards you; give the "down" command as he approaches the proper position. Repeat several times: moderate reinforcement of this procedure should prove rewardingly successful.

For the dog that responds with anger or aggression, attach a lead (and a muzzle) and have the dog sit facing you at a close distance. There should be a J-loop formed by the lead. With moderate force, relative to the size and strength of your dog, step on the J-loop, forcing the dog down, while repeating the command "down" in a low forceful tone. When the dog is down, moderate praise should be given. If the dog proves responsive, you may attempt extending his legs to the "down" position—leaving the muzzle on, of course. Daily reinforcement of the training method will soon yield the desired results. The keys to remember are: patience, persistence, and praise.

Behavior Modification

"Problems with the Barking Dog" and "Aggressive Behavior and Dominance" are extracts from the veterinary monograph *Canine Behavior* (a compilation of columns from *Canine Practice,* a journal published by Veterinary Practice Publishing Company).

PROBLEMS WITH THE BARKING DOG

One of the most frequent complaints about canine behavior is barking. Aside from the biting dog, the barking dog is probably the pet peeve of many non-dog owners. I know of at least one city in which owners of dogs that bark excessively, and for which there are complaints on file, are required to take steps to eliminate the barking.

Canine practitioners are drawn into problems with barking when they are asked for their advice in helping an owner come up with a solution or, as a last resort, when they are requested to perform a debarking operation or even euthanasia. In this column I will deal with some of the factors that apparently cause dogs to bark and suggest some corrective approaches.

Barking is, of course, a natural response for many dogs. They have an inherited predisposition to bark as an alarm when other dogs or

Only in the most extreme situations may trainers recommend electric-shock collars for correcting a dog's misbehavior.

people approach their territory. Alarm barking makes many dogs valuable as household watchdogs and is not necessarily undesirable behavior. With a different vocal tone and pattern, dogs bark when they are playing with each other. On occasion dogs have a tendency to bark back at other dogs or join in with other barking dogs.

In addition to inherited barking tendencies, dogs can also learn to bark if the barking is followed, at least sometimes,

Akitas must be as temperamentally sound as they are physically sound. The beauty of these ancient dogs derives from their great strength of mind and body. Ch. Akiko's Great Gatsby of Kinkoh owned by Kevin and Mary Jones.

by a reward. Thus dogs may bark when they wish to come in the house or to get out of a kennel. Some dogs are trained to bark upon hearing the command "speak" for a food reward.

One of the first approaches to take when discussing a barking problem is to determine if the behavior is a manifestation of a natural (inherited) tendency or is learned behavior which has been rewarded in the past.

Can Barking Be Extinguished? Extinction, as a way of eliminating a behavioral problem, may be considered when it is clear that the behavior has been learned and when one can identify the specific

rewarding or reinforcing factors that maintain the behavior.

For example, the dog that barks upon hearing the command "speak" is periodically rewarded with food and praise. If a dog is never, ever given food or praise again when it barks after being told to "speak," it will eventually stop this type of barking. This is the process of extinction and it implies that the behavior must be repeated but never again rewarded.

A more practical example of the possible use of extinction would be in dealing with the dog that apparently barks because, at least occasionally, it is allowed in the house. By not allowing the dog in the house

Muzzles may prevent biting, but the root cause of biting must be extracted if the dog is to live as a trusted member of the human family.

until the barking has become very frequent and loud, the owners may have shaped the barking behavior to that which is the most objectionable. If the dog is never allowed in the house again when barking, the barking should eventually be extinguished—at least theoretically.

How Should Punishment Be Used? Sometimes it is not feasible to attempt to extinguish barking even if it seems to be the case that the behavior was learned. This brings up the advisability of punishment. Clients who seek advice in dealing with a barking problem may already have employed some type of punishment such as shouting at the dog or throwing something at it. That this type of punishment is ineffective is attested to by the fact that the client is seeking advice. By shouting at a dog or hitting, a person interferes with what effect the punishment may have on the behavior itself through the arousal of autonomic reactions and escape attempts or submissive responses by the dog.

The Water Bucket Approach I am rather impressed by the ingenuity of some dog owners in coming up with ways to punish a dog for barking without being directly involved in administering the punishment. One such

Four Paws Quick Fit Muzzles are the most comfortable and humane muzzles for dogs. Allow dogs to drink water while wearing the muzzles. They are made of nylon and are completely washable.

This young Akita is owned by Linda J. Arsenault.

Pet gates are used to confine a dog to certain areas of the house. The dog must learn to accept any such restrictions and not attempt to overcome them.

harried dog owner I talked to, who was also a veterinarian, was plagued by his dog's barking in the kennel commencing at about 1:30 a.m. every night. A platform to hold a bucket of water was constructed over the area of the kennel in which the dog usually chose to bark. Through a system of hinges, ropes, and pulleys, a mechanism was devised so that the dog owner could pull a rope from his bedroom window, dumping a bucket of water on the dog when he started to bark. The bucket was suspended such that once it was dumped, it uprighted itself and the owner could fill it again remotely by turning on a garden hose. After two appropriate dunkings, the dog's barking behavior was apparently eliminated.

In advising a client on the type of punishment discussed above, keep in mind one important consideration. From the time the owner is ready to administer punishment for barking, every attempt should be made to punish all undesirable barking from that point on and not to allow excessively long periods of barking to go unpunished. Thus it may be necessary to keep a dog indoors when away unless the dog will be punished for barking when the owner is gone.

Alternative Responses

Barking dogs are, and probably always will be, one of the enduring problems of dog owners. Barking is relatively effortless, and it is such a natural response for many dogs that it is admittedly hard to eliminate with either punishment or a program of conditioning non-barking. In some instances it may be advisable to forget about eliminating barking and to suggest that the problem be dealt with by changing the circumstances which lead to barking. For example, a dog that barks continuously in the backyard while the owners are away may not bark if left in the house while they are gone. But the problem of keeping the dog in the house may be related to inadequate house training or the

Four Paws repellents are excellent training aids to keep dogs out of forbidden areas. Use indoors on furniture and rugs; outdoor formula for flowerbeds, shrubs and garbage cans.

Akitas are fairly active for dogs of their size. Exercise and fresh air are essentials to a healthy, happy Akita. Owner, Anthony DeMeo.

dog's shedding hair or climbing onto the furniture. It may be easier to correct these latter behavioral problems than it is to change the barking behavior.

AGGRESSIVE BEHAVIOR AND DOMINANCE

Aggressiveness can have many causes. Determining what kind of aggression an animal is manifesting is a prerequisite to successful treatment of the behavior. A frequent problem that is presented to the practitioner is one of aggression related to dominance.

Dogs, which are social animals, have a hierarchal system of dominance within their pack. This predisposition to take a dominant or submissive position relative to fellow canines also occurs in relationship to people. Only in unusual situations would a submissive dog threaten a dominant animal, and almost never would it physically assault its superior. The dominant dog, however, frequently threatens submissive individuals to maintain its position. In a household setting, a person may be the object of threats, and when the person backs off, the dog's position is reassured. The aggressive behavior is also reinforced, and when behavior is reinforced it is likely to recur.

Owners must take an active part in shaping their dog's behavior. Providing a sensible chew device can help alleviate an animal's frustration and thereby eliminate some undersirable behavior. Once a dog has chewed the Gumabone® to this extent, it's time to buy a new one.

Case History The following is a typical case history of a dog presented for aggression stemming from dominance.

Max was a two-year-old intact male Cocker Spaniel. He had been acquired by Mr. Smith, one year prior to his owner's marriage, as a puppy. He liked and was well liked by both Mr. and Mrs. Smith. He frequently solicited and received attention from both people. However, several times over the last few months, Max had snapped at Mrs. Smith and repeatedly growled at her. A detailed anamnesis revealed that such incidents usually occurred in situations where the dog wanted his own way or did not want to be bothered. He would growl if asked to move off a chair or if persistently commanded to do a specific task. He growled if Mrs. Smith came between him and a young female Cocker Spaniel acquired a year ago. He also refused to let Mrs. Smith take anything from his possession. Max never showed any of these aggressive behaviors toward Mr. Smith or strangers. Admittedly he did not have much opportunity to demonstrate such behaviors toward strangers. A description of the dog's body and facial postures and circumstances under which the aggression occurred did not indicate that this was a case of fear-induced aggression, but rather one of

Treats can be effective in shaping behavior and establishing a rapport with your pet.

assertion of dominance.

Mrs. Smith's reaction to the aggression was always to retreat, and, hence, the dog was rewarded for his assertiveness. She had never physically disciplined the dog and was afraid to do so. To encourage her to physically take control of the dog would likely have resulted in her being bitten. The dominance-submissive

This darling Akita pup belongs to Walter and Victoria Donach.

While crates may be used principally for sleeping and traveling, some owners might opt to employ a crate for disciplining a dog, rather like sending a naughty child to his room.

relationship had to be reversed in a more subtle manner.

Instructions to Client Mrs. Smith was instructed to avoid all situations which might evoke any aggressive signs from Max. This was to prevent any further reinforcement of his growling and threats.

Both she and her husband were not to indiscriminately pet or show affection towards the dog. For the time being, if Max solicited attention from Mr. Smith, he was to ignore the dog. Mrs. Smith was to take advantage of Max's desire for attention by giving him a command which he had to obey before she praised and petted him. She was also to take advantage of high motivation levels for other activities whenever such situations arose. Max had to obey a command before she gave him anything—

before she petted him, before she let him out or in, etc.

Mrs. Smith also was to assume total care of the dog and become "the source of all good things in life" for Max. She was to feed him, take him on walks, play with him, etc.

Mrs. Smith also spent 5–10 minutes a day teaching Max simple parlor tricks and obedience responses for coveted food rewards as well as praise. These were entirely fun and play sessions—but within a few days the dog had acquired the habit of quickly responding to commands. And this habit transferred over to the non-game situations.

Results Within a few weeks, Max had ceased to growl and threaten Mrs. Smith in situations that he previously had. He would move out of her way or lie quietly when she would pass by him. She could order him off the furniture and handle the female Cocker Spaniel without eliciting threats from Max.

Mrs. Smith still felt that she would not be able to take the objects from Max's possession. Additional instructions were given to her. She then began placing a series of objects at progressively closer distances to the dog while the dog was in a sit-stay position. After she placed the object on the floor for a short time, she would pick it up. If the dog was still in a sit-stay (which it always was), he received a reward of cheese and verbal praise. Eventually the objects were to be placed and removed from directly in front of the dog. At first she was to use objects that the dog did not care much about and then progressively use more coveted items. This was what she was supposed to do, but before she actually had completed the program she called in excitedly to report that she had taken a piece of stolen food and a household ornament from Max's mouth. And he didn't even object! She said she had calmly told Max to sit. He did. He was so used to doing so, in the game and other situations, that the response was now automatic. She walked over, removed the item from his mouth, and praised him.

Mrs. Smith did resume the systematic presentation of objects and put the dog on an intermittent schedule of food and praise reinforcement during the practice sessions. Mr. Smith again began interacting with Max.

A progress check six months later indicated Max was still an obedient dog and had definitely assumed a submissive position relative to both of his owners. The dominance hierarchy between Max and Mrs. Smith had been reversed *without resorting to any physical punishment.* Mrs. Smith was instructed to reinforce her dominance position by frequently giving Max a command and reinforcing him for the appropriate response.

Summary The essential elements in treatment of such cases are as follows. First, of course, there must be a correct diagnosis of what kind of aggressive behavior is occurring. During the course of treatment, the submissive person(s) should avoid all situations that might evoke an aggressive attitude by the dog. All other family members should totally ignore the dog during the treatment interim. The person most dominated by the dog should take over complete care of the dog in addition to spending 5–10 minutes a day teaching the dog tricks or simple obedience commands (sit-stay is a useful one to gain control of the dog in subsequent circumstances). These should be fun-and-games situations. Food rewards are highly recommended in addition to simple praise.

The person submissive to the dog should take the opportunity to give the dog a command, which must be obeyed, before doing anything pleasant for the dog.

Four Paws offers Bitter Lime in two ways. A pump spray to stop fur biting and a gel to stop chewing of furniture. Both are safe and non-toxic.

It must be emphasized to the owner that no guarantee can be made that the dog will never threaten or be aggressive again. What is being done, as with all other aggression cases, is an attempt to reduce the likelihood, incidence, and intensity of occurrence of the aggressive behavior.

Old discardable shoes should not be included in the dog's toy box. Such items are dangerous to a puppy or an adult dog.

DESTRUCTIVE TENDENCIES

It is ironical but true that a dog's destructive behavior in the home may be proof of his love for his owner. He may be trying to get more attention from his owner or, in other cases, may be expressing his frustration at his owner's absence. An abundance of unused energy may also contribute to a dog's destructive behavior, and therefore the owner should ensure that his dog has, at least, twenty minutes of vigorous exercise a day.

As a dog's destructive tendencies may stem from his desire to get more attention from his owner, the latter should devote specific periods each day to his dog when he is actively interacting with him. Such a period should contain practice obedience techniques during which the owner can reward the dog with his favorite food as well as praise and affection.

Planned departure conditioning is one specific technique which has been used to solve the problem of destructive tendencies in a puppy. It eventually ensures the dog's good behavior during the owner's absence. A series of short departures, which are identical to real departures, should condition the dog to behave well in the owner's absence. How is this to be achieved? Initially, the departures are so short (2–5 minutes) that the dog has no opportunity to be destructive.

The dog is always rewarded for having been good when the owner returns. Gradually the duration of the departures is increased. The departure time is also varied so that the dog does not know when the owner is going to return. Since a different kind of behavior is now expected, it is best if a new stimulus or "atmosphere" is introduced into the training sessions to permit the dog to distinguish these departures as different from previous departures when he was destructive.

This new stimulus could be the sound of the radio or television. The association which the dog will develop is that whenever the "signal" or "stimulus" is on, the owner will return in an unknown period of time and, if the dog has not been destructive, he will be rewarded. As with the daily owner-dog interaction, the food reward is especially useful.

If the dog misbehaves during his owner's absence, the owner should speak sternly to him and isolate him from social contact for at least thirty minutes. (Puppies hate to be ignored.)

Then the owner should conduct another departure of a shorter time and generously reward good behavior when he returns. The owner should progress slowly enough in the program so that once the departure has been initiated, the dog is never given an opportunity to make a mistake.

If planned departures are working satisfactorily, the departure time

There is a wide variety of collars and harnesses available to the dog owner. Talk with your pet shop proprietor to determine which one best satisfies your needs.

may gradually be extended to several hours. To reduce the dog's anxiety when left alone, he should be given a "safety valve" such as the indestructible Nylabone® to play with and chew on.

Health Care

From the moment you purchase your puppy, the most important person in both your lives becomes your veterinarian. His professional advice and treatment will ensure the good health of your pet. The vet is the first person to call when illness or accidents occur. Do *not* try to be your own veterinarian or apply human remedies to canine diseases. However, just as you would keep a first aid kit handy for minor injuries sustained by members of your family at home, so you should keep a similar kit prepared for your pet.

First aid for your dog would consist of stopping any bleeding, cleaning the wound, and preventing infection. Thus your kit might contain medicated powder, gauze bandages, and adhesive tape to be used in case of cuts. If the cut is deep and bleeding profusely, the bandage should be applied very tightly to help in the formation of a clot. A tight bandage should not be kept in place longer than necessary, so take your pet to the veterinarian immediately.

Walking or running on a cut pad prevents the cut from healing. Proper suturing of the cut and regular changing of the bandages should have your pet's wound healed in a week to ten

Bandaging a minor cut on the paw pad is one of many basic first-aid techniques that the dog owner should learn. Thoroughly clean the injury with peroxide and apply an antibiotic. Then place the injured pad in sterile gauze, secure with first-aid tape, and replace daily.

days. A minor cut should be covered with a light bandage, for you want as much air as possible to reach the wound. Do not apply wads of cotton to a wound, as they will stick to the area and may cause contamination.

You should also keep some hydrogen peroxide available, as it is useful in cleaning wounds and is also one of the best and simplest emetics known. Cotton applicator swabs are useful for applying ointment or removing debris from the eyes. A pair of tweezers should also be kept handy for removing foreign bodies from the dog's neck, head or body.

Nearly everything a dog might contract in the way of sickness has basically the same set of symptoms: loss of appetite, diarrhea, dull eyes, dull coat, warm and/or runny nose, and a high temperature. Therefore, it is most important to take his temperature at the first sign of illness. To do this, you will need a rectal thermometer which should be lubricated with petroleum jelly. Carefully insert it into the rectum, holding it in place for at least two minutes. It must be held firmly; otherwise there is the danger of its being sucked up into the rectum or slipping out, thus giving an inaccurate reading. The normal temperature for a dog is between 101° and 102.5°F. If your pet is

Four Paws Crystal Eye is a safe product for the removal of ugly tear stains.

seriously ill or injured in an accident, your veterinarian will advise you what to do before he arrives.

SWALLOWING FOREIGN OBJECTS

Most of us have had experience with a child swallowing a foreign object. Usually it is a small coin; occasionally it may be a fruit pit or something more dangerous. Dogs, *as a general rule,* will not swallow anything which isn't edible. There are, however, many dogs that swallow pebbles or small shiny objects such as pins, coins, and bits of cloth and plastic. This is especially true of dogs that are offered so-called "chew toys."

Chew toys are available in many sizes, shapes, colors and materials. Some even have whistles which sound when the dog's owner plays with it or when the dog chomps on it quickly. Most dogs attack the whistle first, doing everything possible to make it stop squeaking. Obviously, if the whistle is made of metal, a dog

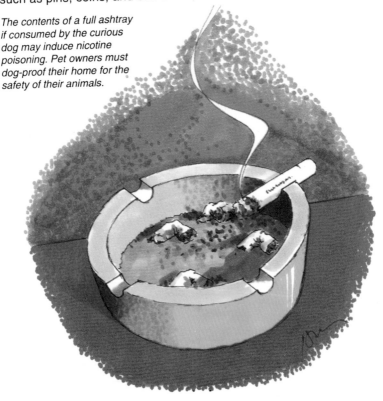

The contents of a full ashtray if consumed by the curious dog may induce nicotine poisoning. Pet owners must dog-proof their home for the safety of their animals.

When emergencies occur, being prepared pays off. A first-aid kit should be accessible and always well stocked with medical accessories and supplies.

can injure its mouth, teeth, or tongue. Therefore, *never* buy a "squeak toy" made with a metal whistle.

Other chew toys are made of vinyl, a cheap plastic which is soft to the touch and pliable. Most of the cute little toys that are figures of animals or people are made of this cheap plastic. They are sometimes hand-painted in countries where the cost of such labor is low. Not only is the paint used dangerous to dogs, because of the lead content, but the vinyl tears easily and is usually destroyed by the dog during the first hour. Small bits of vinyl

may be ingested and cause blockage of the intestines. You are, therefore, reminded of these things before you buy anything vinyl for your dog!

Very inexpensive dog toys, usually found in supermarkets and other low-price venues, may be made of polyethylene. These are to be avoided completely, as this cheap plastic is, for some odd reason, attractive to dogs. Dogs destroy the toy in minutes and sometimes swallow the indigestible bits and pieces that come off. Most pet shops carry only safe toys.

WHAT TOYS ARE SAFE FOR DOGS?

Hard Rubber Toys made of hard rubber are usually safe for dogs, providing the toy is made of 100% hard rubber and not a compound of rubber and other materials. The rubber must be "virgin" and not re-ground from old tires, tubes, and other scrap rubber products. The main problem with rubber, even 100% virgin rubber, is that it oxidizes quickly, especially when subjected to the ultraviolet rays of the sun and a dog's saliva. The rubber then tends to be brittle, to crack, to dust off, and to be extremely dangerous to dogs that like swallowing things.

Nylon Toys Toys made of nylon could well be the safest of all toys, *providing the nylon is annealed.* Nylon that is not annealed is very fragile, and if you smash it against a hard surface, it might shatter like glass. The same is true when the weather is cold and the nylon drops below freezing. Thus far there is only one line of dog toys that is made of annealed virgin nylon—Nylabone®. These toys not only are annealed but they are flavored and scented. The flavors and scents, such as hambone, are undetectable by humans, but dogs seem to find them attractive.

Some nylon bones have the

The Plaque Attacker® is a Dental Ball™, not just a plaything, designed to reduce plaque and tartar by use of its revolutionary "dental tips."

flavor sprayed on them or molded into them. These cheaper bones are easy to detect—just smell them. If you discern an odor, you know they are poorly made. The main problem with the nylon toys that have an odor is that they are not annealed and they "smell up" the house or car. The dog's saliva dilutes the odor of the bone, and when he drops it on your rug, this odor attaches itself to the rug and is quite difficult to remove.

The Puppy Bone® by Nylabone® is multi-purpose: designed for teething, chew-pacification, teeth-cleaning and the elimination of behavioral problems before they become habitual.

Gumabone® is available in different sizes and shapes. These are probably the most popular of all chew toys because dogs love them.

Annealed nylon may be the best there is, but it is not 100% safe. The Nylabone® dog chews are really meant to be Pooch Pacifiers®. This trade name indicates the effect intended for the dog, which is to relieve the tension in your excited puppy or anxious adult dog. Instead of chewing up the furniture or some other object, he chews up his Nylabone® instead. Many dogs ignore the Nylabone® for weeks, suddenly attacking it when they have to relieve their doggie tensions.

The Nylabone® is designed for the most aggressive chewers. Even so, owners should be wary that some dogs may have jaws strong enough to chomp off a piece of Nylabone®, but this is extremely rare. *One word of caution:* the Nylabone® should be replaced when the dog has chewed down the knuckle. Most dogs slowly scrape off small slivers of nylon which pass harmlessly through their digestive tract. The resultant frizzled bone actually becomes a toothbrush.

One of the great characteristics of nylon bones is that they can be boiled and sterilized. If a dog loses interest in his Nylabone®, or it is too hard for him to chew due to his age and the condition of his teeth, you can cook it in some chicken or beef broth, allowing it to boil for 30 minutes. Let it cool down normally. It will then be perfectly sterile and re-flavored for the next dog. *Don't try this with plastic bones, as they will melt and ruin your pot.*

Polyurethane Toys Because polyurethane bones such as the Gumabone® are constructed of

Plaque Attacker™ Dental Bones from Gumabone® are designed for maximum tartar reduction for the aggressive chewer.

the strongest *flexible* materials known, some dogs (and their owners) actually prefer them to the traditional nylon bones. There are several brands on the market: ignore the ones which have scents that you can discern. Some of the scented polyurethane bones have an unbearable odor after the scent has rubbed off the bone and onto your rug or car seat. Again, look for the better-quality polyurethane toy. Gumabone® is a flexible material, the same as used for making artificial hearts and the bumpers on automobiles, thus it is strong and stable. It is not as strong as Nylabone®, but many dogs like it because it is soft.

If your dog is soft-mouthed and a less aggressive, more playful chewer, he will love the great taste and fun feel of the Gumabone® products.

The most popular of the Gumabone® products made in polyurethane are the tug toys, knots, balls, and Frisbee® flying discs. These items are almost clear in color, have the decided advantage of lasting a long time, and are useful in providing exercise for both a dog and his master or mistress.

Made of a more flexible material than nylon, Gumabone® devices often are more appealling to dogs.

Gumabone® has also introduced new spiral-shaped dental devices under the name Plaque Attacker®. These unique products are fast becoming standards for all aggressive chewers. The Plaque Attacker Dental Device® comes in four fun sizes and each is designed to maximize gum and teeth massage through its upraised "dental tips," which pimple the surface of the toy. Similarly, the Plaque Attacker Dental Ball® ensures a reduction in plaque and tartar. This one-of-a-kind product provides hours of fun for a dog. It bounces erratically and proves to be the most exciting of all polyurethane toys. All Plaque Attacker® products are patented and scented with hambone to make them even more enticing for the dog. Clinical findings

The Plaque Attacker™ Dental Ball® is a unique and challenging toy for dogs big and small.

support the assertion that a significant reduction in calculus accompanies use of the Gumbone® products.

Whatever dog toy you buy, be sure it is high quality. Pet shops and certain supermarkets, as a rule, always carry the better-quality toys. Of course there may be exceptions, but you are best advised to ask your local pet shop operator—or even your veterinarian—what toys are suitable for *your* dog.

In conclusion, if your dog is a swallower of foreign objects, don't give him anything cheap to chew on. If he swallows a coin, you can hardly blame the Treasury! Unless your dog is carefully supervised, use only the largest size Nylabone® and Gumabone®, and replace them as soon as the dog chews down the knuckles. *Do not let the dog take the Nylabone® outdoors.* First of all he can hide and bury it, digging it up when his tensions rise. Then, too, all nylon becomes more brittle when it freezes, even Nylabone®.

IF YOUR PET SWALLOWS POISON

A poisoned dog must be treated instantly; any delay could cause his death. Different poisons act in different ways and require different treatments. If you know the dog has swallowed an acid, alkali, gasoline, or kerosene, do not induce vomiting. Give milk to dilute the poison and rush him to the vet. If you can find the bottle or container of poison, check the label to see if there is a recommended antidote. If not, try to induce vomiting by giving him a mixture of hydrogen peroxide and water. Mix the regular drugstore strength of hydrogen peroxide (3%) with an equal part of water, but do not attempt to

Four Paws offers three pleasantly scented colognes that can be used in between baths to freshen up pets.

pour it down your dog's throat, as that could cause inhalation pneumonia. Instead, simply pull the dog's lips away from the side of his mouth, making a pocket for depositing the liquid. Use at least a tablespoonful of the mixture for every ten pounds of your dog's weight. He will vomit in about two minutes. When his stomach has settled, give him a teaspoonful of Epsom salts in a little water to empty the intestine quickly. The hydrogen peroxide, on ingestion, becomes oxygen and water and

is harmless to your dog; it is the best antidote for phosphorus, which is often used in rat poisons. After you have administered this emergency treatment to your pet and his stomach and bowels have been emptied, rush him to your veterinarian for further care.

DANGER IN THE HOME

There are numerous household products that can prove fatal if ingested by your pet. These include rat poison,

143

Wasps can be harmful to dogs and humans alike. Paper wasps often build their nests close to the ground, where a dog may happen to visit.

antifreeze, boric acid, hand soap, detergents, insecticides, mothballs, household cleansers, bleaches, de-icers, polishes and disinfectants, paint and varnish removers, acetone, turpentine, and even health and beauty aids if ingested in large enough quantities. A word to the wise should be sufficient: what you would keep locked away from your two-year-old child should also be kept hidden from your pet.

There is another danger lurking within the home among the household plants, which are almost all poisonous, even if swallowed in small quantities. There are hundreds of poisonous plants around us, among which are: ivy leaves, cyclamen, lily of the valley, rhododendrons, tulip bulbs, azalea, wisteria, poinsettia leaves, mistletoe, daffodils, delphiniums, foxglove leaves, the jimson weed—we cannot name them all. Rhubarb leaves, for example, either raw or cooked, can cause death or violent convulsions. Peach, elderberry, and cherry trees can cause cyanide poisoning if their bark is consumed.

There are also many insects that can be poisonous to dogs

such as spiders, bees, wasps, and some flies. A few toads and frogs exude a fluid that can make a dog foam at the mouth—and even kill him—if he bites too hard!

There have been cases of dogs suffering nicotine poisoning by consuming the contents of full ashtrays which thoughtless smokers have left on the coffee table. Also, do not leave nails, staples, pins, or other sharp objects lying around. Likewise, don't let your puppy play with plastic bags which could suffocate him. Unplug, remove, or cover any electrical cords or wires near your dog. Chewing live wires could lead to severe mouth burns or death. Remember that an ounce of prevention is worth a pound of cure: keep all potentially dangerous objects out of your pet's reach.

VEHICLE TRAVEL SAFETY

A dog should never be left alone in a car. It takes only a few minutes for the heat to become unbearable in the summer, and to drop to freezing in the winter.

A dog traveling in a car or truck should be well behaved. An undisciplined dog can be deadly in a moving vehicle. The dog should be trained to lie on the back seat of the vehicle. Allowing your dog to stick its head out of

Car safety is a serious matter. When a dog is traveling by auto, specially designed seat belts (or the dog's crate) are the safest route.

AMF

Four Paws Pet Safety Sitter is designed to protect pets from injury by securing them in place and preventing them from disturbing drivers and passengers.

the window is unwise. The dog may jump or it may get something in its eye. Some manufacturers sell seat belts and car seats designed for dogs.

Traveling with your dog in the back of your pick-up truck is an unacceptable notion and dangerous to all involved.

PROTECT YOURSELF FIRST

In almost all first aid situations, the dog is in pain. He may indeed be in shock and not appear to be suffering, until you move him. Then he may bite your hand or resist being helped at all. So if you want to help your dog, help yourself first by tying his mouth closed. To do this, use a piece of strong cloth four inches wide and three feet long, depending on the size of the dog. Make a loop in the middle of the strip and slip it over his nose with the knot under his chin and over the bony part of his nose. Pull it tight and bring the ends back around his head behind the ears and tie it tightly, ending with a bow knot for quick, easy release. Now you can handle the dog safely. As a dog perspires through his tongue, do not leave the "emergency muzzle" on any longer than necessary.

ADMINISTERING MEDICINE

When you are giving liquid medicine to your dog, it is a good idea to pull the lips away from the side of the mouth, form a lip pocket, and let the liquid trickle past the tongue. Remain at his side, never in front of the dog, as he may cough and spray you with the liquid. Moreover, you must never pour liquid medicine while the victim's tongue is drawn out, as inhalation pneumonia could be the disastrous result.

Medicine in pill form is best administered by forcing the dog's mouth open, holding his head back, and placing the capsule as far back on his tongue as you can reach. To do this: put the palm of your hand over the dog's muzzle (his foreface) with your fingers on one side of his jaw, your thumb on the other. Press his lips hard against his teeth while using your other hand to pull down his lower jaw. With your two fingers, try to put the pill

as far back on the dog's tongue as you can reach. Keep his mouth and nostrils closed and he should be forced to swallow the medicine. As the dog will not be feeling well, stroke his neck to comfort him and to help him swallow his medicine more easily. Do keep an eye on him for a few moments afterward, however, to make certain that he does not spit it out.

IN CASE OF AN ACCIDENT

It is often difficult for you to assess the dog's injuries after a road accident. He may appear normal, but there might be

Choose from a variety of ear care products from Four Paws from cleaners to remedies for proper ear hygiene.

internal hemorrhaging. A vital organ could be damaged or ribs broken. Keep the dog as quiet and warm as possible; cover him with blankets or your coat to let his own body heat build up. Signs of shock are a rapid and weak pulse, glassy-eyed appearance, subnormal temperature, and slow capillary refill time. To determine the last symptom, press firmly against the dog's gums until they turn white. Release and count the number of seconds until the gums return to their normal color. If it is more than 2–3 seconds, the dog may be going into shock. Failure to return to the reddish pink color indicates that the dog may be in serious trouble and needs immediate assistance.

If artificial respiration is required, first open the dog's mouth and check for obstructions; extend his tongue and examine the pharynx. Clear his mouth of mucus and blood and hold the mouth slightly open. Mouth-to-mouth resuscitation involves holding the dog's tongue to the bottom of his mouth with one hand and sealing his nostrils with the other while you blow into his mouth. Watch for his chest to rise with each inflation. Repeat every 5–6 seconds, the equivalent of 10–12 breaths a minute.

If the veterinarian cannot come to you, try to improvise a stretcher to take the dog to him. To carry a puppy, wrap him in a blanket that has been folded into several thicknesses. If he is in shock, it is better to pick him up by holding one hand under his chest, the other under the hindquarters. This will keep him stretched out.

It is always better to roll an injured dog than to try and lift him. If you find him lying beside the road after a car accident, apply a muzzle even if you have to use someone's necktie to make one. Send someone for a blanket and roll him gently onto it. Two people, one on each side, can make a stretcher out of the blanket and move the dog easily.

If no blanket is available and the injured dog must be moved, try to keep him as flat as possible. So many dogs' backs are broken in car accidents that one must first consider that possibility. However, if he can move his hind legs or tail, his spine is probably not broken. Get medical assistance for him immediately.

It should be mentioned that unfortunate car accidents, which can maim or kill your dog, can be avoided if he is confined at all times either indoors or, if out-of-doors, in a fenced-in yard or some other protective enclosure. *Never* allow your dog to roam free; even a well-trained dog may, for some unknown reason,

VACCINATION SCHEDULE	
Age	**Vaccination**
6-8 weeks	Initial canine distemper, canine hepatitis, tracheobronchitis, canine parvovirus, as well as initial leptospirosis vaccination.
10-12 weeks	Second vaccination for all given at 6-8 weeks. Initial rabies and initial Lyme disease to be given at this time.
14-16 weeks	Third vaccination for all given at 6-8 and 10-12 weeks.Re-vaccinate annually, hereafter. Second rabies and second Lyme disease to be given at this time, and then re-vaccinated annually.

Vaccination schedules should be confirmed with your vet.

dart into the street—and the result could be tragic.

If you need to walk your dog, leash him first so that he will be protected from moving vehicles.

PROTECTING YOUR PET

It is important to watch for any tell-tale signs of illness so that you can spare your pet any unnecessary suffering. Your dog's eyes, for example, should normally be bright and alert, so if the haw is bloodshot or partially covers the eye, it may be a sign of illness or irritation. If your dog has matter in the corners of his eyes, bathe them with a mild eye wash; obtain ointment or eye drops from your veterinarian to treat a chronic condition.

If your dog seems to have something wrong with his ears which causes him to scratch at them or shake his head, cautiously probe the ear with a cotton swab. An accumulation of wax will probably work itself out. Dirt or dried blood, however, is indicative of ear mites or infection and should be treated immediately. Sore ears in the summer, due to insect bites, should be washed with mild soap and water, then covered with a soothing ointment and wrapped in gauze if necessary. Keep your

Mosquitoes are the vectors of disease; although males like this one do not bite, females can transmit heartworm and other diseases to dogs.

pet away from insects until his ears heal, even if this means confining him indoors.

INOCULATIONS

Periodic check-ups by your veterinarian throughout your puppy's life are good health insurance. The person from whom your puppy was purchased should tell you what inoculations your puppy has had and when the next visit to the vet is necessary. You must make certain that your puppy has been vaccinated against the following infectious canine diseases:

distemper, canine hepatitis, leptospirosis, rabies, parvovirus, and parainfluenza. Annual "boosters" thereafter provide inexpensive protection for your dog against such serious diseases. Puppies should also be checked for worms at an early age.

DISTEMPER

Young dogs are most susceptible to distemper, although it may affect dogs of all ages. Some signs of the disease are loss of appetite, depression, chills, and fever, as well as a watery discharge from the eyes and nose. Unless treated promptly, the disease goes into advanced stages with infections of the lungs, intestines, and nervous system. Dogs that recover may be impaired with paralysis, convulsions, a twitch, or some other defect, usually spastic in nature. Early inoculations in puppyhood should be followed by an annual booster to help protect against this disease.

CANINE HEPATITIS

The signs of hepatitis are drowsiness, loss of appetite, high temperature, and great thirst. These signs may be accompanied by swellings of the head, neck, and abdomen. Vomiting may also occur. This disease strikes quickly, and death may occur in only a few hours. An annual booster shot is needed after the initial series of puppy shots.

LEPTOSPIROSIS

Infection caused by either of two serovars, *canicola* or *copehageni,* is usually begun by the dog's licking substances contaminated by the urine or feces of infected animals. Brown rats are the main carriers of *copehageni.* The signs are weakness, vomiting, and a

Biting bugs not only have a painful bite but also carry blood parasites.

yellowish discoloration of the jaws, teeth, and tongue, caused by an inflammation of the kidneys. A veterinarian can administer the bacterins to protect your dog from this disease. The frequency of the doses is determined by the risk factor involved.

RABIES

This disease of the dog's central nervous system spreads by infectious saliva, which is transmitted by the bite of an infected animal. Of the two main classes of signs, the first is "furious rabies," in which the dog shows a period of melancholy or depression, then irritation, and finally paralysis. The first period can be from a few hours to several days, and during this time the dog is cross and will change his position often, lose his appetite, begin to lick, and bite or swallow foreign objects. During this phase the dog is spasmodically wild and has impulses to run away. The dog acts fearless and bites everything in sight. If he is caged or confined, he will fight at the bars and possibly break teeth or fracture his jaw. His bark becomes a peculiar howl. In the final stage, the animal's lower jaw becomes paralyzed and

Heartworm life cycle: a carrier mosquito bites a dog and deposits microfilariae, which travel through the dog's bloodstream, lodging in the heart to reproduce. The carrier dog is later bitten by an uninfected mosquito, which becomes infected, and bites and infects another dog...

hangs down. He then walks with a stagger, and saliva drips from his mouth. About four to eight days after the onset of paralysis, the dog dies.

The second class of symptoms is referred to as "dumb rabies" and is characterized by the dog's walking in a bearlike manner with his head down. The lower jaw is paralyzed and the dog is unable to bite. It appears as if he has a bone caught in his throat.

If a dog is bitten by a rabid animal, he probably can be saved if he is taken to a veterinarian in time for a series of injections. After the signs appear, however, no cure is possible. The local health department must be notified in the case of a rabid dog, for he is a danger to all who come near him. As with the other shots each year, an annual rabies inoculation is very important. In many areas, the administration of rabies vaccines for dogs is required by law.

Lice are not a common problem in dogs and usually only infest dogs that are poorly cared for. Proper care of your dog will prevent lice infestation.

PARVOVIRUS

This relatively new virus is a contagious disease that has spread in almost epidemic proportions throughout certain sections of the United States. It has also appeared in Australia, Canada, and Europe. Canine parvovirus attacks the intestinal tract, white blood cells, and heart muscle. It is believed to spread through dog-to-dog contact, and the specific course of infection seems to come from fecal matter of infected dogs. Overcoming parvovirus is difficult, for it is capable of existing in the environment for many months under varying conditions and temperatures, and it can be transmitted from place to place streaked. Because of the vomiting and severe diarrhea, the dog that has contracted the disease will dehydrate quickly. Depression and loss of appetite, as well as a rise in temperature, can accompany the other symptoms. Death caused by this disease usually occurs within 48 to 72 hours following the appearance of the symptoms. Puppies are hardest hit, and the virus is fatal to 75 percent of puppies that contract it. Death in puppies can be within two days of the onset of the illness.

A series of shots administered by a veterinarian is the best preventive measure for canine parvovirus. It is also important to disinfect the area where the dog is housed by

Four Paws Protector Flea & Tick Spray offers a quick kill and will repel fleas for up to 14 days. Super Fly Repellent repels flies and mosquitoes, which are known to transmit heartworm.

on the hair and feet of infected dogs, as well as on the clothes and shoes of people.

Vomiting and severe diarrhea, which will appear within five to seven days after the animal has been exposed to the virus, are the initial signs of this disease. At the onset of illness, feces will be light gray or yellow-gray in color, and the urine might be blood-

using one part sodium hypochlorite solution (household bleach) to 30 parts of water and to keep the dog from coming into contact with the fecal matter of other dogs.

LYME DISEASE

Known as a bacterial infection, Lyme disease is transmitted by ticks infected with a spirochete known as *Borrelia burgdorferi*. The disease is most often acquired by the parasitic bite of an infected deer tick, *Ixodes dammini*. While the range of symptoms is broad, common warning signs include: rash beginning at the bite and soon extending in a bullseye-targetlike fashion; chills, fever, lack of balance, lethargy, and stiffness; swelling and pain, especially in the joints, possibly leading to arthritis or arthritic conditions; heart problems, weak limbs, facial paralysis, and lack of tactile sensation.

Concerned dog owners, especially those living in the United States, should contact a veterinarian to discuss Lyme disease. A vaccination has been developed and is routinely administered to puppies twice before the 16th week, and then repeated annually.

PARAINFLUENZA

Parainfluenza, or infectious canine tracheobronchitis, is commonly known as "kennel cough." It is highly contagious, affects the upper respiratory system, and is spread through direct or indirect contact with already diseased dogs. It will readily infect dogs of all ages that have not been vaccinated or that were previously infected. While this condition is definitely one of the serious diseases in dogs, it is self-limiting, usually lasting only two to four weeks. The symptoms are high fever and intense, harsh coughing that brings up mucus. As long as

The fraternity of internal parasites and their eggs: whipworms, hookworms, roundworms and tapeworms.

your pet sees your veterinarian immediately, the chances for his complete recovery are excellent.

EXTERNAL PARASITES

A parasite is an animal that lives in or on an organism of another species, known as the host, without contributing to the well-being of the host. The majority of dogs' skin problems are parasitic in nature and an estimated 90% of puppies are born with parasites.

Ticks can cause serious problems to dogs where the latter have access to woods, fields, and vegetation in which large numbers of native mammals live. Ticks are usually found clinging to vegetation and attach themselves to animals passing by. They have eight legs and a heavy shield or shell-like covering on their upper surface. Only by keeping dogs away from tick-infested areas can ticks on dogs be prevented.

The flea is the single most common cause of skin and coat problems in dogs. There are 11,000 kinds of fleas which can transmit specific disorders like tapeworm and heartworm or transport smaller parasites onto your dog. The common tapeworm, for example, requires the flea as an intermediate host for completion of its life cycle.

A female flea can lay hundreds of eggs and these will become adults in less than three weeks. Depending on the temperature and the amount of moisture, large numbers of fleas can attack dogs. The ears of dogs, in particular, can play host to hundreds of fleas.

Fleas can lurk in crevices and cracks, carpets, and bedding for months, so frequent cleaning of your dog's environment is absolutely essential. If he is infected by other dogs, then have him bathed and "dipped," which means that he will be put into water containing a chemical that kills fleas. Your veterinarian will advise which dip to use, and your dog must be bathed for at least twenty minutes.

INTERNAL PARASITES

Four common internal parasites that may infect a dog are: roundworms, hookworms, whipworms, and tapeworms. The first three can be diagnosed by laboratory examination of the dog's stool, and tapeworms can be seen in the stool or attached to the hair around the anus. When a veterinarian determines what type of worm or worms are present, he then can advise the best treatment.

Roundworms, the dog's most common intestinal parasite, have a life cycle which permits complete eradication by worming twice, ten days apart. The first worming will remove all adults and the second will destroy all subsequently hatched eggs before they, in turn, can produce more parasites.

A dog in good physical condition is less susceptible to worm infestation than a weak dog. Proper sanitation and a nutritious diet help in preventing worms. One of the best preventive measures is to have clean, dry bedding for the dog, as this diminishes the possibility of reinfection due to flea or tick bites.

Heartworm infestation in dogs is passed by mosquitoes. Dogs with this disease tire easily, have difficulty in breathing, and lose weight despite a hearty appetite. Administration of preventive medicine throughout the spring, summer, and fall months is advised. A veterinarian must first take a blood sample from the dog to test for the presence of the disease, and if the dog is heartworm-free, pills or liquid medicine can be prescribed to protect against any infestation.

CANINE SENIOR CITIZENS

The processes of aging and gradual degenerative changes start far earlier in a dog than often observed, usually at about seven years of age. Your pet will become less active, will have a poorer appetite with increased thirst, there will be frequent periods of constipation and less than normal passage of urine. His skin and coat might become dull and dry and his hair will become thin and fall out. There is a tendency towards obesity in old age, which should be avoided by maintaining a regular exercise program. Remember, also, that your pet will be less able to cope with extreme heat, cold, fatigue, and change in routine.

There is the possibility of loss or impairment of hearing or eyesight. He may become bad-tempered more often than in the past. Visits to the vet should be more regular. Care of the teeth is also important in the aging dog. Indeed, the mouth can be a barometer of nutritional health. Degenerating gums, heavy tartar on the teeth, loose teeth, and sore lips are common. The worst of all diseases in old age, however, is neglect. Good care in early life will have its effect on your dog's later years; the nutrition and general health care of his first few years can determine his lifespan and the quality of his life. It is worth bearing in mind that the older, compared to the younger, animal needs more protein of good biological value, more vitamins A, B-complex, D and E, more calcium and iron, less fat and fewer carbohydrates.

The Dog Show World

Quality in the sense of "show quality" is determined by various factors such as the dog's health, physical condition, temperament, ability to move, and appearance. Breeders trying to breed show dogs are attempting to produce animals which come as close as possible to the word description of perfection as set out in the breed standard.

Keep in mind that dog show terminology varies from one place to another and even from one time to another. If you plan to show your dog, it always makes sense to check with your local or national breed club or with the national dog registry for the most complete, most up-to-date information regarding dog show regulations. In Great Britain, for example, match shows are known as limit shows. Age limit also differs, as dogs less than six months old may not be shown in Britain. Additionally, Britain has no point system for dogs, rather the dogs compete for championship certificates (C.C.s). Thus, point shows are known as championship shows in Great Britain.

MATCH SHOWS

One of the best ways to see if your puppy has championship potential is to attend a match show which is usually organized by the local kennel club or breed specialty club. Such shows provide a useful learning experience for the amateur and they offer you the opportunity to see how well your dog measures up to others being shown. There you can mingle with owners and professional handlers and pick up basic guidelines in showmanship, performance, and procedure. You can learn a great deal merely by closely observing the professional handlers performing in the ring.

The age limit is usually reduced to two months at match shows so that puppies can have four months of training before they compete in the regular shows when they reach six months. This time also helps them to overcome any "crowd nervousness." As class categories are the same as those included at a regular show, much experience can be gained in this informal atmosphere. Entry fees are low and paid at the door.

Before you go to a show, your dog should be trained to gait at a trot beside you, with head up and in a straight line. In the ring you will have to gait

Facing page: The most prestigious dog show in America is the Westminster Kennel Club Show held annually in Madison Square Garden, New York City.

around the edge with other dogs and then individually up and down the center runner. In addition, the dog must stand for examination by the judge, who will look at him closely and feel his head and body structure. He should be taught to stand squarely, hind feet slightly back and head up. He must hold the pose when you place his feet, and he must show a lively interest when you "bait" him, i.e., tempt him with a piece of boiled liver or a small squeak toy.

If your puppy receives praise and words of encouragement from the judges and other knowledgeable people, then you can begin to dream of Westminster or Crufts. It is always useful to visit such prestigious shows to see the best examples of all the various breeds.

After you have taken some handling lessons yourself, or employed a professional handler, the next step is participation in the point shows where you can earn points toward your dog's championship.

POINT SHOWS

Unlike match shows where your dog was judged on ring behavior, at point shows he will be judged on conformation to his breed standard. It is advisable to write to your national dog registry for information on how to register your dog and apply to dog shows. Below are the names and addresses of registries in the United States, Canada, Great Britain, and Australia.

The American Kennel Club
51 Madison Avenue
New York, NY 10010

The Canadian Kennel Club
111 Eglinton Avenue
East Toronto, Ontario M6S 4V7
Canada

The Kennel Club
1 Clarges Street Piccadilly,
London, W1Y 8AB, England

The Australian Kennel Club
Royal Show Grounds
Ascot Vale, Victoria, Australia.

Your local kennel club can provide you with the names and addresses of the show-giving superintendents (or show secretaries) near you, who will be staging the club's dog show for them, and where you must write for an official entry form. The forms will be mailed in a pamphlet called the "premium list" which will include the names of the judges for each breed, a list of the prizes and trophies, the names and addresses of the show-giving club, where the show will be held, as well as the rules and required procedure. Make certain that you fill in the form clearly and carefully and

Responsible breeders of Akitas devote much time to training and showing their dogs. The show ring has long been a testing ground for the future outstanding sires and dams of each breed. Owner, Windom Akitas.

Four Paws offers an extensive line of grooming brushes, from slickers to curry brushes to pin brushes. These are sure to suit the grooming needs of every dog.

mail it in plenty of time.

Before then, however, you will have to decide in which classes your dog should compete. In the United States these are: Puppy, Novice, Bred-by-Exhibitor, American-bred and Open.

Puppy Classes are for dogs six months of age and over but under twelve months which are not champions. The age of a dog shall be calculated up to and inclusive of the first day of the show.

The *Novice Class* is for dogs six months of age and over, whelped in the United States or Canada, which have not, prior to the official closing date for entries, won three first prizes in the Novice Class, a first prize in Bred-by-Exhibitor, American-bred or Open Class or one or more points toward championship. In Britain, of course, dogs competing in the Novice Class must have been whelped in Britain.

The *Bred-by-Exhibitor Class*

is for dogs whelped in the U.S.A. or, if individually registered in the American Kennel Club Stud Book, for dogs in Canada that are six months of age and over. They must not be champions (although they may be in Britain), and must be owned wholly or in part by the person or the spouse of the person who was the breeder or one of the breeders of record. Dogs in this class must be handled by an owner or by a member of the immediate family of the owner. (This is not the case, however, in Britain.) Members of an immediate family for this purpose are: husband, wife, father, mother, son, daughter, brother and sister. This class has been referred to as the "breeder's showcase" as it is the one where the breeders can be justly proud of their achievements. The

American-bred Class is for all dogs (except champions) six months of age or over, whelped in the U.S.A. by reason of a mating that took place in the U.S.A.

The *Open Class* is for any dog six months of age or over, except in a member specialty club show held only for American-bred dogs, in which

The Shed 'N Blade is a tool used by groomers and handlers to eliminate dead, unwanted hair and allow for a healthy and vibrant coat.

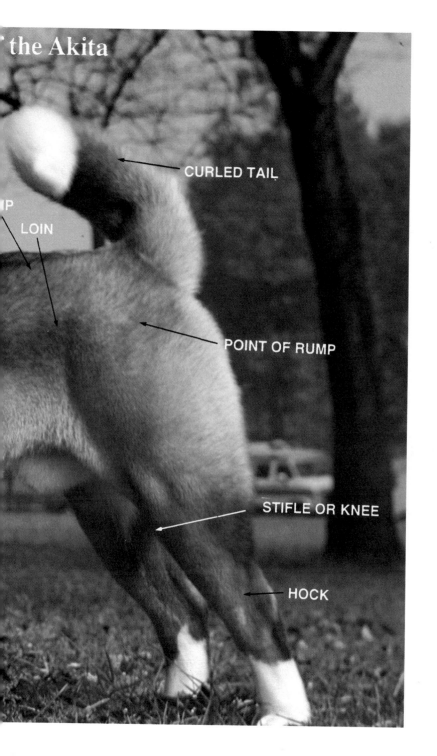

the Akita

CURLED TAIL

P

LOIN

POINT OF RUMP

STIFLE OR KNEE

HOCK

case the class is for American-bred dogs only.

In the United States and Canada, one does not enter the *Winners Class.* One earns the right to compete in it by winning first prize in one of the above classes. Winners Dog and Winners Bitch are the awards which carry points toward championship with them. Also

designated by the judge are the Reserve Winners Dog and the Reserve Winners Bitch (in Britain these are designated Reserve C.C. Dog and Reserve C.C. Bitch) but they do not receive any points. This award means simply that the dog or bitch receiving it are standing "in reserve" should the Winners Dog or Winners Bitch be disallowed through any technicality in the official show rules and regulations.

The dog and bitch then compete against each other for Best of Winners, and they also vie with the champions in the

Specials Class for Best of Breed and for Best of Opposite Sex to Best of Breed. In Britain, the Reserve C.C. winners compete against each other for Best of Breed, not Best of Winners.

Best of Breed is the highest-placing dog in a given breed, and that winner then represents the particular breed in Group competition. Groups include: 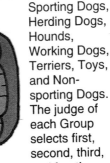 Sporting Dogs, Herding Dogs, Hounds, Working Dogs, Terriers, Toys, and Non-sporting Dogs. The judge of each Group selects first, second, third, and fourth place among the Best of Breed winners within specific Groups. First-place winners in each Group then compete for Best in Show.

A scale of points is printed in each dog-show catalog, and the number of points awarded in a breed depends on the number of dogs shown in competition. A win of three or more points at a show is called a "major." To attain championship, a dog must win a total of fifteen points under at least three different judges, and included in those fifteen points must be two majors (each under a different judge). A dog that accumulates fifteen points and no majors does not qualify for championship. A dog must win in keen competition. (This is the case in the United States but not in Great Britain. As there is no point system in Britain, it doesn't matter how many dogs are shown in competition. Championship Certificates are awarded at the discretion of the judge, however few dogs are competing.)

OBEDIENCE AND FIELD TRIALS

It should be mentioned that obedience trials, in which any purebred dog may compete, are often held in conjunction with conformation shows. Dogs are judged on performance rather than on how well they measure up to their breed standard. Many dogs that have already earned their championship in the conformation ring also compete for obedience trial degrees.

Two training accessories especially common with obedience trial enthusiasts are the hurdle (below) and the dumbbell (facing page). To see dogs performing with these and other field accessories, attend an obedience competition. Remember that training requires consistency and commitment, but the rewards are well worth the effort.

Akitas can be shown in any color or pattern. Generally speaking, Akitas do not enjoy the show ring and must be acclimated at an early age.

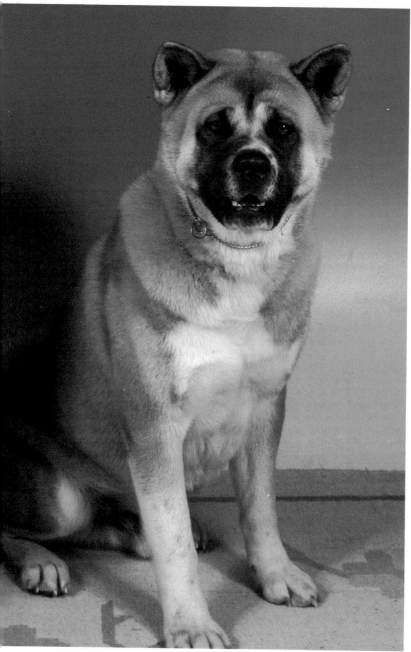

Akitas have a reputation of being defiant and head strong, thus making obedience training an absolute must. Owner, Brenda Ament.

Some breeds, particularly hunting dogs and some of the hounds, also compete in field trials.

There are three classes in obedience: Novice, Open, and Utility. Tracking tests also are held. The respective degrees earned are: C.D., C.D.X., U.D., and T.D. These are: Companion Dog, Companion Dog Excellent, Utility Dog, and Tracking Dog. To earn a C.D., both the dog and his handler must perform six exercises together to the satisfaction of three different judges. Judges score the teams on a scale of zero to 200 points, and a score of 170 points or higher earns a dog a "leg" toward his obedience degree. A dog must achieve three "legs" for a C.D. Exercises in this Novice Class are: heel on lead and figure eight, stand for examination by a judge, heel off lead, long sit (sitting for a required number of minutes), long down (being down for several minutes), and recall (returning to his owner when called). After a dog gets his C.D., he then may try for his C.D.X. in Open obedience where he must jump over obstacles, retrieve items, and do more difficult exercises in three different trials. To achieve a U.D. title, a dog must do directed retrieving, jumping, and scent discrimination. To obtain a tracking degree, a dog competes in field trials where he "tracks" or follows a scent.

PRE-SHOW PREPARATIONS

As a very basic guide, the following list has been compiled to help you with your preparations for your first point show: the identification ticket sent by the show superintendent, a grooming table, a sturdy tack box in which to carry your dog's grooming tools, a leash to fasten him to the bench or stall and another show lead, your first aid kit, packaged "dog treats," and a supply of food and water for man and beast. Take the largest thermos you can find and a water dish. Remember to feed your dog after the show, not before, and make certain that he exercises and relieves himself before he enters the ring. Many experts think that an exercise pen is mandatory to eliminate the risk of exposing your dog to any diseases in the common exercise ground at shows, but before you bring one along, check the show rules to see if these are allowed. Moreover, exercise pens are useful as places where your dog can stretch out or rest during your travels or at a motel.

Even take time to think about what you are going to wear on the big day; sports clothes and

AMERICAN DOG SHOW JUDGING PROCEDURE

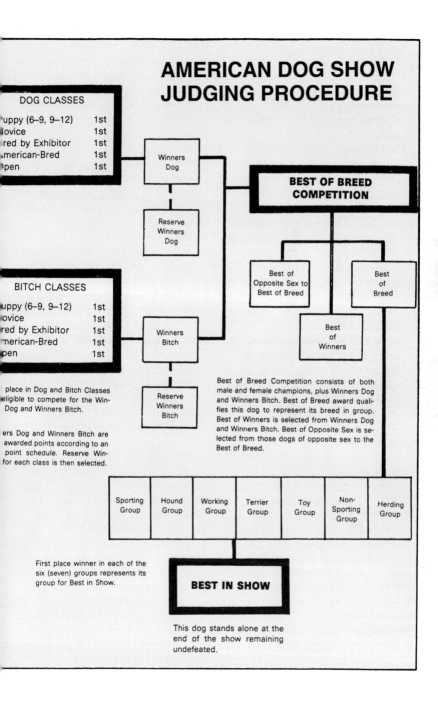

DOG CLASSES

Puppy (6–9, 9–12)	1st
Novice	1st
Bred by Exhibitor	1st
American-Bred	1st
Open	1st

Winners Dog

Reserve Winners Dog

BITCH CLASSES

Puppy (6–9, 9–12)	1st
Novice	1st
Bred by Exhibitor	1st
American-Bred	1st
Open	1st

Winners Bitch

Reserve Winners Bitch

place in Dog and Bitch Classes eligible to compete for the Winners Dog and Winners Bitch.

ers Dog and Winners Bitch are awarded points according to an point schedule. Reserve Winfor each class is then selected.

BEST OF BREED COMPETITION

Best of Opposite Sex to Best of Breed

Best of Breed

Best of Winners

Best of Breed Competition consists of both male and female champions, plus Winners Dog and Winners Bitch. Best of Breed award qualifies this dog to represent its breed in group. Best of Winners is selected from Winners Dog and Winners Bitch. Best of Opposite Sex is selected from those dogs of opposite sex to the Best of Breed.

Sporting Group	Hound Group	Working Group	Terrier Group	Toy Group	Non-Sporting Group	Herding Group

First place winner in each of the six (seven) groups represents its group for Best in Show.

BEST IN SHOW

This dog stands alone at the end of the show remaining undefeated.

Akitas participating in the breed ring. Always try to stack your dog to his best advantage.

low-heeled, comfortable shoes are the best. You certainly do not want to wear anything that would distract the judge's attention from your dog; you should merely provide an attractive background for him.

Although your knees may be trembling, try to appear self-confident as you gait (move) and set up the dog. The judging routine usually begins when the judge asks that the dogs be gaited in a circle around the ring while he observes their style, topline, head and tail carriage, reach and drive, and general balance. Avoid going too close to the dog in front of you. Make certain that the judge has an unrestricted view of your dog by keeping him on the inside of the circle, between you and the judge.

DOG SHOW ETIQUETTE

There are a few "golden rules" to be followed at dog shows which are worth mentioning at this stage. First of all, you are responsible for the behavior of your dog at all times. Keep your dog with you until the showing and keep him under control at all times. Constant vigilance is necessary as thefts have been known at dog shows, as well as poisoning and physical abuse of the animals by jealous exhibitors. You do not want your dog to become involved in a dog fight or taken for a walk by an irresponsible child or one too young to discipline him. In other words, you must not let your dog out of your sight.

Another golden rule is to be punctual; do not be late for your class. Remember that in the ring

Dog show exhibitors must be prepared to supervise and clean up after their dogs whenever on show grounds.

Squeaky toys and fuzzy animals are excellent tools to bait a dog in the show ring. Be sure not to distract your dog when the judge is examining him.

you must not communicate with the judge or fellow competitors. Watch the judge carefully and follow his instructions. Bear in mind that the ring is not the place to discipline or train your dog; it is too late at this stage! Whatever the judge's decision, accept it with good grace whether you win or lose. *Never* argue with a judge. Finally, remember to praise your dog for his efforts. It has been a long day for him as well.

"DOUBLE HANDLING"

Only one person should be handling your dog; there should not be other "handlers" in the audience who hope to influence his performance by the well-timed whistle, the "spontaneous" applause, or the secret signal. Such tactics are unsportsmanlike as they often distract the attention of other dogs. This so-called "double handling" is frowned upon by the American Kennel Club as a desperate measure resorted to by a desperate owner. Moreover, to try to prompt a win or stir up interest in your dog by bringing along your own cheering section is a futile gesture as a judge is concentrating on what he is doing and is not influenced by such subversive strategy. These people seem to be declaring that their dog cannot win by its own merits under normal conditions but needs some extra assistance.

Breeders often photograph litters so that potential owners can see how the pups are developing. Coloration on the pups changes with time and ears sometimes take longer to erect. Owners, Brian and Cassi Belli.

Owner Concerns

By Chris Walkowicz

If something's worth doing at all, it's worth doing right. Behind the scenes of every gourmet feast, there's a lot of work, time and expense. Someone has to handle messy clean-up chores as well. The same is true of any worthwhile effort: a prize-winning novel, a community play, a good marriage, children, pets.

Conscientious owners know that there's more to raising a dog than picking one out, feeding it once a day and petting it if they feel the urge. Just as a fancy restaurant includes fine linens, flowers on the table and an attractive ambiance with the sustenance, being a top-quality dog owner means more than tossing a bone in the backyard now and then.

STRAYS

Although some people still have the mistaken idea that "a dog must be free," most are discovering that the world isn't what it once was. Loose dogs enjoying their "freedom" face all kinds of traumas: shotguns, poison, traps, oncoming trucks, dog pounds and the resulting euthanasia.

A dog without a home can rarely find a handout or even a rabbit to run down anymore. Garbage forays don't go far enough to fill an empty stomach, and they anger the person who is left to pick up the mess. Cars take their tolls on the highways. To combat these and other problems, good owners are taking steps to make sure their dogs remain welcome in society.

When a breeder is first contacted by a prospective buyer, the question is not simply, "Do you have a fenced yard?" but "Do you have a pen or a fenced yard—or do you plan to walk your dog on leash?" No option. If "none of the above" is the answer, it's bye-bye, buyer.

Children who are uncontrolled and unrestricted are obnoxious, cause damage and are a danger to themselves. Responsible people know that when they tell their children "No," it really is for their own good and that of others. It's not just a power ploy to deny them a privilege. Although it is difficult, there are reasons parents deny complete freedom to children, and there are reasons to deny it to dogs.

Dogs will be dogs. Loose animals are, at the least, a pain in the posterior and, at worst, a threat to themselves and others. Stray dogs bite, poop, scare kids, chase people, strew garbage, ruin lawns and gardens, kill other animals and produce unwanted litters.

OVERPOPULATION

The number of once-upon-a-time pets humanely euthanized annually in pounds and shelters is mind-boggling. These and the additional number of animals who die in agony—starvation, abuse, disease, trauma or road kills—were murdered by irresponsible owners and breeders as surely as if they aimed a gun and pulled the trigger. If animals were considered as living creatures instead of property by the court systems, many owners could be charged with negligence in their pets' deaths.

Neutering (spaying and castrating) means fewer animals, and fewer animals enable us to decrease the horrible statistics. Not only do we ascertain that none of our dog's pups become part of the canine carnage, but neutering also lowers the percentage of cancers and diseases of the reproductive system.

There are already plenty of dogs in the world without creating more. Anyone who wants one can find one immediately. It's only when people want specifics (i.e., a Pointer with great hunting ability; a Saint Bernard with lines that are hip-certified and show longevity; a Dachshund pup with the potential to go Best in Show) that someone needs to supply a demand.

It is true that a mixed-breed dog can make a great pet. Any dog, even one whose background is unknown, might turn into your best pal. But you're taking your chances. There are already thousands of those to go around—no need to create more. Only someone who cares enough to obtain the knowledge to produce canines with specific physical characteristics, temperament and instincts has a right to add to the already-bulging and suffering canine population. Therefore, ethical breeders now sell companion pups with a spay/neuter clause, which requires the dog to be neutered at puberty or by the age of one year. Many also use the Limited Registration option with the American Kennel Club. This allows the dog itself to be registered and shown in obedience and instinct tests, but in case of a "mistake," none of its progeny can be registered.

Dog breeding, done properly, is an expensive proposition. It is also time-consuming, extra work, occasionally heartbreaking and often frustrating. Add all of these problems to the fact that a neutered pet is a healthier one, many pet—and even some show—owners now choose a sexless life for their dog.

LICENSING

Dog licenses are not another means to extract more money from your pocket for the local government, but rather they are

Responsible owners must take care that their dogs and puppies are properly identified as well as registered with the national kennel club. Akitas owned by Anthony DeMeo and Bill and Mary Richardson.

insurance for your dog. A dog license just might save your pet from euthanasia. Animal control officers compare the dog license to our own driver's licenses. It's an I.D. That tag hanging from his collar can be traced to the owner, which means a lost pet might be saved from the gas chamber. Licenses also contribute toward the care of the unwanted, forgotten and forlorn ex-pets who will pay the price for "freedom."

THEFT AND LOSS

It's terrifying when a dog owner first looks outdoors and sees the empty yard with the gate swinging open. When someone realizes his pet is gone, the heart takes a plummeting ride to the pit of the stomach.

Sometimes, no matter what precautions are taken, accidents happen—a child leaves a gate open or a well-behaved dog finds a rabbit on the other side of the fence too attractive to resist.

Owners should take action immediately to assure the pet's return. Don't wait a few hours to see if he'll come home. It may be too late.

To find a lost dog:

1. POSTERS—Have hundreds printed at a jiffy printer, preferably with a photo, and post every one. Someone who sees one poster may not retain the memory, but someone who sees 20 will remember. Describe the dog, always keeping in mind the fable of the blind men and the elephant. To a large man, a medium-sized dog may appear to be small; to a child, it may seem to be an elephant. In addition, a lost dog usually loses weight. It's better to print a lower estimate of his size and describe the breed, even if it's a well-known breed. Remember if the dog is gone for more than a few hours, a well-groomed animal can quickly become disheveled and appear unkempt.

2. SPREAD THE WORD—Tell the mail carrier (who's always on the alert for stray dogs). Call the neighbors and schools (kids enjoy helping and love dogs). Call the police, veterinarians, pounds, shelters and humane societies not only in your county but in the surrounding counties. Dogs travel many miles in search of the cat they spied . . . or home. Not all dogs have the homing instinct of Lassie. As soon as possible, visit animal organizations with your posters. Don't take their word that there is no such purebred on the premises. Most people wouldn't recognize one if it bit them—and then it would probably be too late.

3. ADVERTISE—Call the papers and the radio stations. Offer a reward (which should also be

printed on the posters). Make it high enough to make it worthwhile for someone to return the dog, but low enough that it does not invite extortionists.

4. SEARCH—Never stop searching. Use an answering machine or have someone stay by the phone to answer any reports of the dog being sighted. Dogs have been found as long as six months after their loss.

5. HUMANE TRAP—Set a familiar object (a blanket or a crate with a favorite toy) on your porch or in your garage, along with bowls of food and water. If he does come home while you're out searching, he'll have a reason to stay.

6. PREVENTION—Fences, kennel runs and walking on leash. If the dog is a jumper or climber, make the fence higher or plant shrubs around to increase the distance and top the run. I.D. your dog with tags and a tattoo. Take photos, both *haute coiffure* and *au naturel.*

7. BE PREPARED—A lost dog is often terrified. Even those who are normally friendly can panic when called by a stranger, or even by someone they've known and loved all their lives. Use a lure: food, a kennelmate, an open car door, a bitch in season for a stud dog, a favorite toy or sound (like food pans, or a gunshot for a hunting dog).

Too often, also, dognappers are lured by a winsome face,

easy prey, or the potential easy money flashed by a purebred. The dognapper's booty is sometimes sold to people who are unaware of the circumstances. Most times, however, they're marketed to dog brokers, who fake papers and resell the dog. Worse yet, they might be sold to dog fighters (as bait or fighters) or laboratories (for experiments). Stolen dogs are difficult, if not impossible, to trace unless they can be positively identified.

TATTOO IDENTIFICATION

To prevent a much-loved family pet from ending his days in fear and agony, the best method of prevention is tattooing. Many dog clubs and veterinarians provide tattoo identification. By law, no laboratory may use a dog bearing a tattoo. Although some owners tattoo on the inside of the ear, most choose the inside of the rear thigh. An ear can be easily cut off.

Most American owners use their social security number, which is usually put on the inside of the dog's right hind thigh. Some use the dog's registration number, which goes on the inside of the left rear thigh. The area is first shaved and numbed. There is no pain, although a few dogs do not like the buzzing sound.

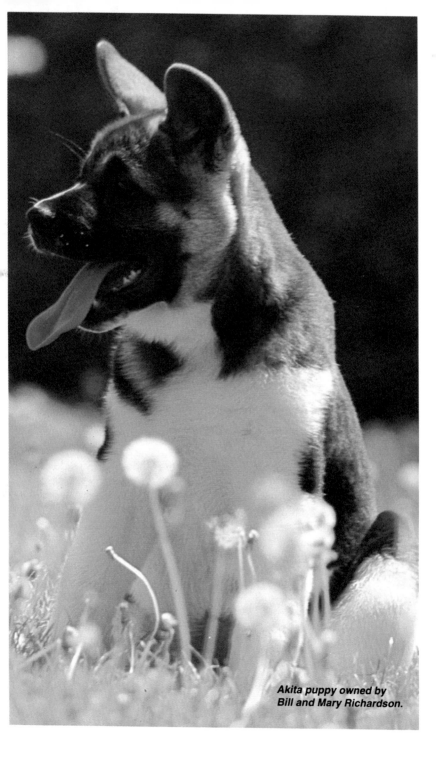

*Akita puppy owned by
Bill and Mary Richardson.*

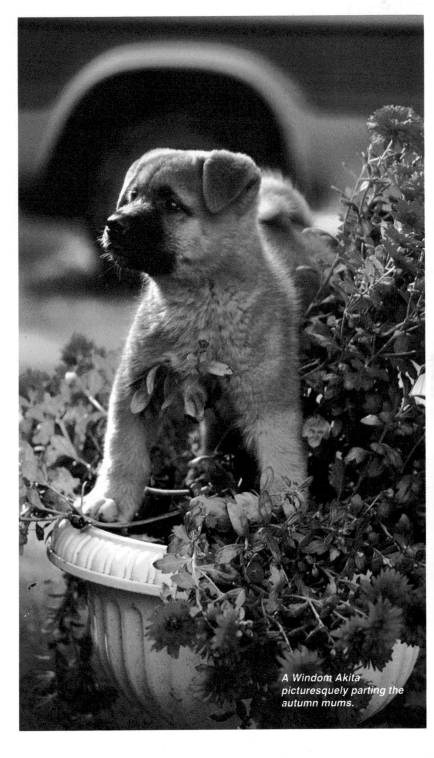

A Windom Akita picturesquely parting the autumn mums.

A number may be registered for a fee with the National Dog Registry (NDR), Box 116, Woodstock, NY 12498, 914-679-BELL or 800-NDR-DOGS. NDR also sponsors an organization for pets of the elderly or financially disadvantaged who have pets in need of emergency care. The NDR Rescue Fund is aided by donations.

Other registries are the Breeder's Action Board, 15870 Allen Road, Taylor, MI 48180, 313-285-6311; I.D. Pet, Inc., 74 Hoyt Street, Darien, CT 06820, 203-327-3157 or 800-243-9147; Tattoo-A-Pet, 1625 Emmons Avenue, Brooklyn, NY 11235, 718-646-8200 or 800 TAT-TOOS. The American Kennel Club contacts the owner of record for dogs tattooed with AKC numbers, phone 919-493-7396.

Another recent method of identification is implantation of a microchip. Information may be obtained from INFOPET, 5137 N. Clareton, Suite 110, Agoura Hills, CA 91301, 800-INFOPET.

NO DOGS!

In Europe, dogs accompany their masters everywhere—to stores, buses and even in restaurants. Because the dogs are accustomed to public acceptance, they're well behaved and sit or lie quietly. Or is it because the pets are well behaved that they are accepted?

In the United States, however, "No Dogs"! signs are popping up like weeds—all over and too many. Because of bratty canines and careless owners, landlords demand a no-pets clause in leases. Parks restrict certain areas for pets if they're allowed at all. Many motels and hotels no longer admit anyone with a dog.

Many cities have a poop-scoop ordinance. Owners are required to clean up after their dogs or pay a fine. For too long, people have had the mistaken notion that their bad habits are not offensive to others, or even if they are, that's tough luck. These people claim, "It's our right to leave doggy doo-doo (drive carelessly, be sloppy drunk, blow smoke in your face or you fill in the blank). We aren't hurting anyone." Wrong. It's our right to own dogs but not to turn parks, sidewalks and public places into doggy latrines. Now we know our bad habits can be not only offensive but harmful to others, and we've got to straighten up and fly right, or we'll be flying solo.

If we want to continue this special bond between dogs and people, we must scoop poop, walk dogs on leash and train them to behave in public. It's no longer a good idea but a necessity that we attend classes and practice good manners. That demands confining pets and curtailing barking. It means no destruction of motel rooms, no jumping up when uninvited and no disgusting piles left behind— in other words, cleaning up our act.

RESCUE

Dog fanciers have recognized the need to spread good will beyond the home boundaries. There are too many strays, abuse cases and abandoned animals. Dogs in these situations need help, and they can't supply it themselves. Their so-called owners won't supply it.

Local and national clubs have organized rescue associations to aid in placing these needy dogs. Members volunteer to investigate situations, check out shelters and even to house a victim temporarily. Because of conditions where the animals may have suffered physically as well as mentally, many dogs need TLC and veterinary treatment before a new home is sought. Usually the dog is neutered before placement. Occasionally, there is a waiting list for "orphans of the storm." Other times, a dog must be maintained and made well again before being adopted. All prospective homes are thoroughly screened so that the tragedy does not reoccur.

Medical care, boarding,

adoption fees, transportation and routine expenses all mean that breed rescue programs need funds. Some samaritans foot the bills themselves. Clubs hold fundraising occasions which include bake sales, garage sales, recycling, tattoo clinics, auctions, matches, dog washes and dips and a rescue "check-off" included with the check for annual dues. Recipients of rescued dogs often respond and are, in some cases, required to make donations.

When these dogs are once again sound, they are placed in good homes. In this way, club members feel they are giving something back to the breed they love so much.

Breeders can assist in assuring that their pups won't someday be in need of rescue by including return clauses in their contracts. The breeder should always have first option to take the dog back if he needs to be placed. Follow up on pups with inquiries to see how they're doing, requests for photos to fill the breeder's scrapbook, and suggestions of training classes. Offering your assistance to groom or handle the dog and your availability to answer questions will help the new owner make it through tough times and offer assurance that one of your pups won't become a victim of our throw-away society.

Breeders aim for consistency of type from generation to generation. Ideally a breeder can see improvements in his line with each new litter. Owners, Steven and Miriam Lisker.

VICIOUS DOGS

A dog bite is painful. The animal should be punished and so should the owner. Punishment should be based on the severity of the bite, whether the animal has a past record of aggression and the individual situation, such as provocation or misguided protection.

The "pit bull" scare has brought to light the urgency of owner responsibility. The English have a saying, "The virtues of a dog are its own, its vices those of its master."

No generic condemning of a breed or breeds will solve the problem. Only enforcement of existing leash and confinement laws will resolve it, along with strict fines for the owner and, in cases of repeated bites, removal and destruction of the dog.

In 1991 a Dangerous Dog Act was enacted in England targetted at fighting dogs (including pit bulls and other breeds with "like characteristics"). As a result, dogs labelled dangerous must be muzzled in public, may not be sold, exchanged, given away or abandoned—and of course must not be bred.

The American Kennel Club has been instrumental in encouraging proper legislation against dangerous dogs without specifying the breed. Breed specific legislation punishes innocent dogs and owners just because they fit the (oftentimes vague) description, and it allows a dog who is not one of the "wanted" to escape punishment.

SHIPPING

Whether for a move, a dog show, breeding or vacation, owners occasionally must ship their pets by air. Loss, discomfort, missed connections, worry for the owner, a frightened pet, even death of the animal— all of these are major concerns for the person considering air shipment of a dog.

Various precautions can help assure your pet's safety. Buy a shipping crate, available from airlines, pet suppliers and pet stores. The crate is two pieces made from durable, molded plastic, held together by nuts and bolts. Because these sometimes loosen, particularly after use, examine for tightness. Bungee cords can also be used to secure the crate in both directions. When shipping puppies, shredded computer paper makes a soft bed and is more absorbent and less messy than a blanket in case of a "goof." A favorite toy covered with your scent will be comforting. Acclimate the dog to a crate prior to the shipping date. Label the crate with the dog's name (in case of a mishap, calling a dog by name helps), owner's name, address and phone. A health certificate must be obtained within ten days of the shipping date. Most veterinarians do not advise tranquilizing the animal as it may disorient them.

Toy dogs may be carried on board in a small (7.5 inch) crate which is placed under the seat. Airline regulations state that the dog must remain in the crate. Reservations must be made at least a week in advance for shipping, whether in cabin, excess baggage (accompanied by a passenger) or as air freight. Ship nonstop or direct, if possible, and avoid shipping on weekends or using two different airlines. If this must be done, check with the flight attendant at each stop.

The dog should not be fed for eight hours prior to shipment, and unless it's extremely warm, water should be withheld for the last couple hours before the flight. A bowl can be attached to the inside of the kennel door so that chips of ice, water or kibble can be dropped in without opening the door. Walk the dog immediately before placing him in the crate for loading.

Although airline regulations stipulate that no animals may be shipped when the temperature is below 10°F or -12°C (others say 35°F or 1°C) or above 85°F or 30°C, a warm rug is soothing during cold weather, and

insulated cold packs under a damp towel help during warm spells.

Depending on the size of the airport, the dog must arrive at baggage one or two hours before the flight. When you arrive, buy additional insurance. It doesn't hurt for the ground crew to realize they're handling valuable cargo. Verify with the flight crew that your dog is safely on the plane. Check and double check.

PUPPY MILLS

The best puppy mill or puppy farm cannot possibly offer the care and attention that a hobby breeder can. The sheer numbers prevent that. Puppy mill profiteers boast of placing 300 puppies a week! Adding the adult dogs, even with a staff of ten, that's less than three minutes a working day per dog—barely enough to feed and clean up. Socialization and cuddling must be sacrificed, even if the caretakers like dogs. Face it, would we like animals if all we did was put food in one end and clean it up from the other?

Certainly, niceties such as evaluating temperament and personalities, matchmaking new owners with pups, introduction to grooming and leash training cannot possibly be squeezed into the day. These "high-class" businesses occasionally have a veterinarian they work with.

Quality puppies are well adjusted and biddable; they should be healthy and hearty and of course look like Akitas. Owners, Brian and Cassi Belli

Other times, they diagnose and medicate dogs themselves. Breeding stock is never tested for congenital and hereditary conditions, i.e., hip dysplasia, cataracts or deafness.

Pedigrees are iffy. Registration papers are as good as the owner's word. Sometimes two males are with the bitch. Sometimes one male services everybody of that breed, daughters, sisters, mother. This is the best of the puppy mills.

The worst dispenses with the amenities. Dogs live in small pens or chicken coops their entire lives, with feet never touching the ground. Some, kept inside, never see light and go blind. Waste piles up underneath the grating which serves as a floor to the pens. When such premises are raided, the animals panic when they are touched or if they are placed on the ground. They're wormy, mangy, undernourished and full of fleas and maggots.

Water is scarce, ventilation poor and sanitation unheard of. They're fed the poorest food, sometimes scraps, sometimes nothing. In some circumstances, they have been forced to cannibalize each other when one starves. Carcasses lie where they drop until there is time or the inclination to haul them out and dispose of them.

Bitches are bred on the first season and every one thereafter. They pay their way or they die. When bitches stop producing or their litters decrease in numbers, they're killed, usually shot. Sometimes the first shot doesn't kill them. But since bullets cost money, sometimes the castaways lie there until they die.

Puppies are shipped as soon as they're weaned, so that no unnecessary expense is invested in the product. If they are weaned, it may be on bread and milk or scraps. The only medication that is given is that which is required by law.

The problem with even the best of these operations is that they think of a dog as produce. Profit is the only motive.

On a farm, food stock such as cattle and hogs produce meat, milk, butter, eggs or leather. Dogs, however, are themselves the end product. The buyers have to live with all the psyches and physical conditions caused by the birth environment.

Animals who are kept in this environment don't live, they only exist . . . and not for long. Perhaps the saddest thing is that the great devotion and loyalty that is instinctive in dogs is never tapped. . . and certainly never returned.

WHAT CAN WE DO?

1. Spay pets so that one of our pups will never end his days

193

in a chamber of horrors.

2. Learn which questions to ask to determine whether the breeder is in it for love or money.

3. Examine the premises and ask to see the parents or at least the dam of the litter.

4. Don't buy on impulse—compare. Go on gut feeling. If you sense something is wrong, get out.

5. Educate yourself about the breed, then ask to see health certification papers for hips, eyes or specific conditions that appear in your chosen breed.

6. Don't think that just because a pup has registration papers and a pedigree that it is automatically quality.

7. Pet shop owners who deal in dogs should buy only from local breeders whose premises and animals can be checked out.

8. Demand stricter laws so that all animal abuse and neglect cases will be punished and put out of business.

FOSTER HOMES

What many owners fail to consider, however, is that their pets may outlive them.

Death is not the only thing that can cause separation. Illness, injury or extended hospitalization or nursing home care can mean that we're unable to care for our dogs.

Pet owners should name a caretaker who will take over in case of an emergency. Write all information about your dog in a booklet or type an instruction sheet, covering feeding, medication and medical records. Include a paragraph about the pet's schedule, likes, dislikes, allergies, favorite toys and so on. If there is more than one pet, note a description of each, preferably with a photo. Give a copy to the veterinarian, a neighbor, a relative and the caretaker. Inform the caretaker of travel plans.

Providing for your dog in case of your death is responsible ownership. Allot a sum for his care and note the provisions in a statement of intent which should be attached to your instruction sheet as well as to your will. Waiting for the will to be read could mean a long spell before your dog's next meal.

You may add further provisions, such as neutering or euthanization of an old or sickly pet who may have trouble adjusting or be too much care for another person. Notify your veterinarian of specific wishes.

Breeding

As the owner of a purebred dog, you may have considered breeding your pet at one time or another. If your dog is a beloved family pet, and not a show dog, you should *not* breed your dog. Breeding is not a hobby for pet owners, but rather a demanding, complicated vocation that is not to be dabbled with. Many people have thought of breeding as an easy-money opportunity: buy two dogs and let them do the work. The rule of thumb is: if you're making money by breeding dogs, you're doing something wrong!

Consider the time and money involved just to get your bitch into breeding condition and then to sustain her throughout pregnancy and afterwards while she tends her young. You will be obligated to house, feed, groom, and housebreak the puppies until good homes can be found for them; and, lest we forget, there will be periodic trips to the vet for check-ups, wormings, and inoculations. Common sense should tell you that it is indeed cruel to bring unwanted or unplanned puppies into an already crowded canine world; only negligent pet owners allow this to happen. Recognizing the number of dogs, purebred and mixed breeds, pet-, show- and breeding-quality, that are put to sleep annually, responsible breeders require that all pet animals be neutered. This

condition most often is incorporated into the selling contract. The motives of good breeders are clear: avoid the manufacturing and mass-producing of average and below-average dogs; control the overblown canine population; concentrate on the improvement of purebred bloodlines. Breeding is a noble calling and unless you can improve the breed, you should not consider breeding your animal. Despite all of the obvious virtues of breeding texts, no book could ever prepare a person for breeding. What a heart-breaking and tragic experience to lose an entire litter because a good-intentioned pet owner wasn't aware of potential genetic complications, didn't recognize a breech birth, or couldn't identify the signals of a struggling bitch! Possibly the dam could be lost as well!

Before you take any step towards mating your bitch, think carefully about why you want her to give birth to a litter of puppies. If you feel she will be deprived in some way if she is not bred, if you think your children will learn from the experience, if you have the mistaken notion that you will make money from this great undertaking, think again. A dog can lead a perfectly happy, healthy, normal life without having been mated; in fact, spaying a female and neuterin a male helps them become better, longer-lived pets, as they are not so anxious to search for a mate in an effort to relieve their sexual tensions and have a diminished risk of cancer. As for giving the children a lesson in sex education, this is hardly a valid reason for breeding your dog. And on an economic level, it takes not only years of hard work (researching pedigrees and bloodlines, studying genetics, among other things), but it takes plenty of capital (money, equipment, facilities) to make a decent profit from dog breeding. Why most dedicated breeders are lucky just to break even. If you have only a casual interest in dog breeding, it is best to leave this pastime to those who are more experienced in such matters, those who consider it a serious hobby and a real vocation. If you have bought a breeder– or show-quality canine, one that may be capable of producing champions, and if you are just starting out with this

Breeding dogs requires more than book knowledge. In dogs, breech presentation is not uncommon and the breeder must be prepared to handle this situation and guide the puppy so that neither the pup nor the bitch is injured.

breeding venture, seek advice from the seller of your dog, from other veteran breeders, and from your veterinarian before you begin.

The following sections on reproduction are intended for academic value only. This is not a "How-to" chapter on breeding, nor a step-by-step approach for the novice for getting started. Hopefully the reader will understand the depth and complexity of breeding as well as the expected ethical and moral obligations of persons who

choose to do so—and never attempt it.

THE FEMALE "IN SEASON"

A bitch may come into season (also known as "heat" or estrus) once or several times a year, depending on the particular breed and the individual dog. Her first seasonal period, that is to say, the time when she is capable of being fertilized by a male dog, may occur as early as six months with some breeds. If you own a female and your intention is *not* to breed her, by

Ideally the puppy will be delivered in the normal head-first position.

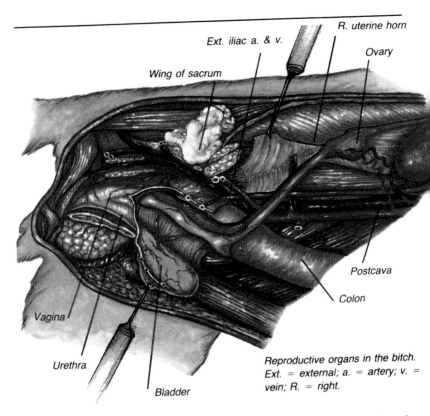

R. uterine horn
Ext. iliac a. & v.
Ovary
Wing of sacrum
Postcava
Colon
Vagina
Urethra
Bladder

Reproductive organs in the bitch.
Ext. = external; a. = artery; v. = vein; R. = right.

The reproductive system of the female dog consists of a highly specialized system of organs situated to the rear of the animal.

all means discuss with the vet the possibility of having her spayed: this means before she reaches sexual maturity.

The first sign of the female's being in season is a thin red discharge, which may increase for about a week; it then changes color to a thin yellowish stain, which lasts about another week. Simultaneously, there is a swelling of the vulva, the exterior portion of the female's reproductive tract; the soft, flabby vulva indicates her readiness to mate. Around this second week or so ovulation occurs, and this is the crucial period for her to be bred, if this is what you have in mind for her. It is during this middle phase of the heat cycle when conception can take place. Just remember that there is great variation from bitch to bitch with regard to how often they come into heat, how long the heat cycles last, how long the period of ovulation lasts, and how much time elapses between heat cycles. Generally, after the third week of heat, the vulval swelling decreases and the estrus period ceases for several months.

It should be mentioned that the female will probably lose her puppy coat, or at least shed part of it, about three months after she has come into season. This is the time when her puppies would have been weaned, had she been mated, and females generally drop coat at this time.

With female dogs, there are few, if any, behavioral changes during estrus. A bitch may dart out of an open door to greet all available male dogs that show an interest in her, and she may occasionally raise her tail and

Each egg within the female is surrounded by a wall that normally takes many sperm to penetrate. In this way, it is more likely that only the strongest sperm will fertilize the egg. A fertile female in season usually has a number of eggs, known as gametes.

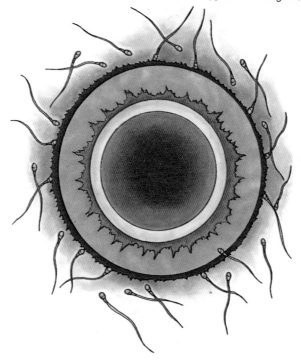

assume a mating stance, particularly if you pet her lower back; but these signs are not as dramatic as those of the sexually mature male. He himself does not experience heat cycles; rather, he is attracted to the female during all phases of her seasonal period. He usually becomes more aggressive and tends to fight with other males, especially over females in heat. He tends to mark his territory with urine to attract females and at the same time to warn other competitive males. It is not uncommon to see him mount various objects, and people, in an effort to satisfy his mature sexual urges.

If you are a homeowner and you have an absolutely climb-proof and dig-proof run within your yard, it may be safe to leave your bitch in season there. But then again it may not be a wise idea, as there have been cases of males mating with females right through chain-link fencing! Just to be on the safe side, shut her indoors during her heat periods and don't let her outdoors until you are certain the estrus period is over. Never leave a bitch in heat outdoors, unsupervised, even for a minute so that she can defecate or urinate. If you want to prevent the neighborhood dogs from hanging around your doorstep, as they inevitably will do when

they discover your female is in season, take her some distance away from the house before you let her do her business. Otherwise, these canine suitors will be attracted to her by the arousing odor of her urine, and they will know instinctively that she isn't far from her scented "calling card." If you need to walk your bitch, take her in the car to a nearby park or field for a chance to stretch her legs. Remember that after about three weeks, and this varies from dog to dog, you can let her outdoors again with no worry that she can have puppies until the next heat period.

If you are seriously considering breeding your dog, first talk to as many experienced breeders as possible and read up on the subject in specific books and articles. Only when you are fully aware of the demands and responsibilities of breeding should you make your final decision. It must be stated here that there is no shortage of fine dogs in need of good homes, nor is there likely to be in the foreseeable future. So, if

Facing page: The male reproductive system includes the penis and testicles. When not excited, the penis is withdrawn into the dog's body.

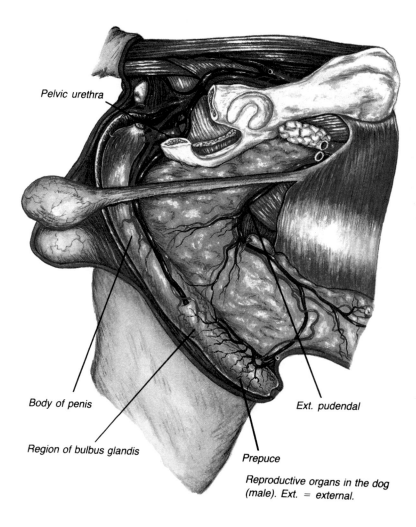

Pelvic urethra

Body of penis

Region of bulbus glandis

Prepuce

Ext. pudendal

Reproductive organs in the dog
(male). Ext. = external.

PERPETUAL WHELPING CHART

	1	2	3	4	5	6	7	8	9	10	11	12	13	14	15	16	17	18	19	20	21	22	23	24	25	26	27	28	29	30	31
Bred—Jan.	1	2	3	4	5	6	7	8	9	10	11	12	13	14	15	16	17	18	19	20	21	22	23	24	25	26	27	28	29	30	31
Due—March	5	6	7	8	9	10	11	12	13	14	15	16	17	18	19	20	21	22	23	24	25	26	27	28	29	30	31	April 1	2	3	4
Bred—Feb.	1	2	3	4	5	6	7	8	9	10	11	12	13	14	15	16	17	18	19	20	21	22	23	24	25	26	27	28			
Due—April	5	6	7	8	9	10	11	12	13	14	15	16	17	18	19	20	21	22	23	24	25	26	27	28	29	30	May 1	2			
Bred—Mar.	1	2	3	4	5	6	7	8	9	10	11	12	13	14	15	16	17	18	19	20	21	22	23	24	25	26	27	28	29	30	31
Due—May	3	4	5	6	7	8	9	10	11	12	13	14	15	16	17	18	19	20	21	22	23	24	25	26	27	28	29	30	31	June 1	2
Bred—Apr.	1	2	3	4	5	6	7	8	9	10	11	12	13	14	15	16	17	18	19	20	21	22	23	24	25	26	27	28	29	30	
Due—June	3	4	5	6	7	8	9	10	11	12	13	14	15	16	17	18	19	20	21	22	23	24	25	26	27	28	29	30	July 1	2	
Bred—May	1	2	3	4	5	6	7	8	9	10	11	12	13	14	15	16	17	18	19	20	21	22	23	24	25	26	27	28	29	30	31
Due—July	3	4	5	6	7	8	9	10	11	12	13	14	15	16	17	18	19	20	21	22	23	24	25	26	27	28	29	30	31	August 1	2
Bred—June	1	2	3	4	5	6	7	8	9	10	11	12	13	14	15	16	17	18	19	20	21	22	23	24	25	26	27	28	29	30	
Due—August	3	4	5	6	7	8	9	10	11	12	13	14	15	16	17	18	19	20	21	22	23	24	25	26	27	28	29	30	31	Sept. 1	
Bred—July	1	2	3	4	5	6	7	8	9	10	11	12	13	14	15	16	17	18	19	20	21	22	23	24	25	26	27	28	29	30	31
Due—September	2	3	4	5	6	7	8	9	10	11	12	13	14	15	16	17	18	19	20	21	22	23	24	25	26	27	28	29	30	Oct. 1	2
Bred—Aug.	1	2	3	4	5	6	7	8	9	10	11	12	13	14	15	16	17	18	19	20	21	22	23	24	25	26	27	28	29	30	31
Due—October	3	4	5	6	7	8	9	10	11	12	13	14	15	16	17	18	19	20	21	22	23	24	25	26	27	28	29	30	31	Nov. 1	2
Bred—Sept.	1	2	3	4	5	6	7	8	9	10	11	12	13	14	15	16	17	18	19	20	21	22	23	24	25	26	27	28	29	30	
Due—November	3	4	5	6	7	8	9	10	11	12	13	14	15	16	17	18	19	20	21	22	23	24	25	26	27	28	29	30	Dec. 1	2	
Bred—Oct.	1	2	3	4	5	6	7	8	9	10	11	12	13	14	15	16	17	18	19	20	21	22	23	24	25	26	27	28	29	30	31
Due—December	3	4	5	6	7	8	9	10	11	12	13	14	15	16	17	18	19	20	21	22	23	24	25	26	27	28	29	30	31	Jan. 1	2
Bred—Nov.	1	2	3	4	5	6	7	8	9	10	11	12	13	14	15	16	17	18	19	20	21	22	23	24	25	26	27	28	29	30	
Due—January	3	4	5	6	7	8	9	10	11	12	13	14	15	16	17	18	19	20	21	22	23	24	25	26	27	28	29	30	31	Feb. 1	
Bred—Dec.	1	2	3	4	5	6	7	8	9	10	11	12	13	14	15	16	17	18	19	20	21	22	23	24	25	26	27	28	29	30	31
Due—February	2	3	4	5	6	7	8	9	10	11	12	13	14	15	16	17	18	19	20	21	22	23	24	25	26	27	28	March 1	2	3	4

your object in breeding is merely to produce more dogs, you are strongly encouraged to reconsider your objective.

WHEN TO BREED

It is usually best to breed a bitch when she comes into her second or third season. Plan in advance the time of year which is best for you, taking into account your own schedule of activities (vacations, business trips, social engagements, and so on). Make sure you will be able to set aside plenty of time to assist with whelping of the newborn pups and caring for the dam and her litter for the next few weeks. At the very least, it probably will take an hour or so each day just to feed and clean up after the brood—but undoubtedly you will find it takes

much longer if you stop to admire and play with the youngsters periodically! Refrain from selling the litter until it is at least six weeks old, keeping in mind that a litter of pups takes up a fair amount of space by then. It will be your responsibility to provide for them until they have been weaned from their mother, properly socialized, housebroken, and ready to go to new homes (unless you plan to keep them all). Hopefully, as strongly recommended, you will have already lined up buyers for the pups in advance of their arrival into this world.

CHOOSING THE STUD

You can plan to breed your female about six-and-one-half months after the start of her last season, although a variation of a

Whelping box prepared with "pig rails," bars on either side of the box to prevent the bitch from rolling on the puppies.

month or two either way is not unusual. Do some research into the various bloodlines within your breed and then choose a stud dog and make arrangements well in advance. If you are breeding for show stock, which will command higher prices than pet-quality animals, a mate should be chosen very carefully. He should complement any deficiencies (bad traits) that your female may have, and he should have a good show record or be the sire of show winners, if he is old enough to have proven himself. If possible, the bitch and stud should have several ancestors in common within the last two or three generations, as such combinations have been known, generally, to "click" best.

The owner of a stud dog usually charges a stud fee for use of the animal's services. This does not always guarantee a litter, but if she fails to conceive, chances are you may be able to breed your female to that stud again. In some instances the owner of the stud will agree to take a "first pick of the litter" in place of a fee. You should, of course, settle all details beforehand, including the possibility of a single puppy surviving, deciding the age at which the pup is to be taken, and so forth.

Each puppy is delivered in a separate membranous sac. This sac must be removed by the bitch without delay—if not, the breeder must come immediately to the assistance of the pup.

If you plan to raise a litter that will be sold exclusively as pets, and if you merely plan to make use of an available male (not a top stud dog), the most important selection point involves temperament. Make sure the dog is friendly, as well as healthy, because a bad disposition can be passed on to his puppies—and this is the worst of all traits in a dog destined to be a pet. If you are breeding pet-quality dogs, a "stud fee puppy," not necessarily the choice of the litter, is the usual payment. Don't breed indiscriminately; be sure you will be able to find good homes for each of the pups, or be sure you have the facilities to keep them yourself, *before* you plan to mate your dog.

PREPARATION FOR BREEDING

Before you breed your female, make sure she is in good health. She should be neither too thin nor too fat. Any skin disease *must* be cured first so that it is not passed on to the puppies. If she has worms, she should be wormed before being bred or within three weeks after the mating. It is generally considered a good idea to revaccinate her against distemper and hepatitis before the puppies are born.

The female will probably be ready to breed twelve days after the first colored discharge appears. You can usually make arrangements to board her with the owner of the stud for a few days, to insure her being there at the proper time; or you can take her to be mated and bring her home the same day if you live near enough to the stud's owner. If the bitch still appears receptive she may be bred again two days later, just to make certain the mating was successful. However, some females never

Newborn pups are very susceptible to chills, so the breeder must dry the puppy off thoroughly and place it in a temperature-controlled puppy box.

show signs of willingness, so it helps to have an experienced breeder on hand. In fact, you both may have to assist with the mating by holding the animals against each other to ensure the "tie" is not broken, that is, to make certain copulation takes place.

Usually the second day after the discharge changes color is the proper time to mate the bitch, and she may be bred for about three days following this time. For an additional week or so, she may have some discharge and attract other dogs by her odor; but she should not be bred.

Once she has been bred, keep her far from all other male dogs, as they have the capacity to impregnate her again and sire some of her puppies. This could prove disastrous where purebred puppies.

THE FEMALE IN WHELP

You can expect the puppies nine weeks from the day of the mating, although 61 days is as common as 63. Gestation, that period when the pups are developing inside their mother, varies among individual bitches. During this time the female should receive normal care and exercise. If she was overweight at the start, don't increase her food right away; excess weight at whelping time can be a problem with some dogs. If she is on the thin side, however, supplement her meal or meals with a portion of milk and biscuit at noontime. This will help build her up and put weight on her.

You may want to add a mineral and vitamin supplement to her diet, on the advice of your veterinarian, since she will need an extra supply not only for herself but for the puppies growing inside her. As the mother's appetite increases, feed her more. During the last two weeks of pregnancy, the pups grow enormously and the mother will have little room for food and less of an appetite. She should be tempted with meat, liver, and milk, however.

As the female in whelp grows heavier, cut out violent exercise and jumping from her usual routine. Although a dog used to such activities will often play with the children or run around voluntarily,

"Pooping" the puppies, or rubbing the bowels and genitals to stimulate elimination, may be necessary if the bitch doesn't tend to this herself.

restrain her for her own sake.

A sign that whelping is imminent is the loss of hair around her breasts. This is nature's way of "clearing a path" so that the puppies will be able to find their source of nourishment. As parturition draws near, the breasts will have swelled with milk and the nipples will have enlarged and darkened to a rosy pink. If the hair in the breast region does not shed for some reason, you can easily cut it short with a pair of scissors or comb it out so that it does not mat and become a hindrance to the suckling pups later on.

The breeder must actively partake in cleaning the pup after feedings. Hands-on contact serves as the initial step in socialization—accustoming the pup to his human family.

PREPARING FOR THE PUPPIES

Prepare a whelping box a few days before the puppies are due, and allow the mother to sleep there overnight or to spend some time in it during the day to become accustomed to it. This way she is less likely to try to have her pups under the front porch or in the middle of your bed. A variety of places will serve, such as the corner of your cellar or garage (provided these places are warm and dry). An unused room, such as a dimly lit spare bedroom, can also serve as the place for delivery. If the weather is warm, a large outdoor dog house will do, as long as it is well protected from rain, drafts, and the cold—and enclosed by fencing or a run. A whelping box serves to separate mother and puppies from visitors and other distractions. The walls should be high enough to restrain the puppies yet low enough to allow the mother to take a short respite from her brood after she has fed them. Four feet square is minimum size (for most dogs) and six-to-eight-inch high walls will keep the pups in until they begin to climb; then side walls should be built up so that the young ones cannot wander away from their nest. As the puppies grow, they really need more over the whole area will make excellent bedding and be absorbent enough to keep the surface warm and dry. These should be removed daily and replaced with another thick layer. An old quilt or washable blanket makes better footing for the nursing puppies than slippery newspaper during the first week; this is also softer for the mother to lie on.

Be prepared for the actual

Bottle-feeding may be necessary with particularly large litters or with a bitch who has become overly stressed or neglectful or whose milk has gone bad.

room anyway, so double the space with a very low partition down the middle of the box, and soon you will find them naturally housebreaking themselves. Puppies rarely relieve themselves where they sleep. Layers of newspapers spread whelping several days in advance. Usually the mother will tear up papers, refuse food, and become restless. These may be false alarms; the real test is her temperature, which will drop to below 100°F (38°C) about twelve hours before whelping. Take her temperature with a rectal thermometer, morning and evening, and usher her to her whelping box when her temperature goes down. Keep a close watch on her and make sure she stays safely indoors (or outdoors in a safe enclosure); if she is let outside, unleashed, or allowed to roam freely, she could wander off and start to go into labor. It is possible that she could whelp anywhere, and this could be unfortunate if she needs your assistance.

WHELPING

Usually little help is needed from you, but it is wise to stay close to be sure that the mother's lack of experience (if this is her first time) does not cause an unnecessary complication. Be ready to help when the first puppy arrives, for it could smother if she does not break the amniotic membrane enclosing it. She should tear open the sac and start licking the puppy, drying and stimulating it. Check to see that all fluids have

Using simple genetic rules, an owner can predict to some degree the traits that the offspring of a given mating can exhibit. The six possible ways in which a pair of determiners can unite are illustrated on this Mendelian expectation chart. Ratios apply to expectancy over large numbers, except in lines 1, 2, and 6 where exact expectancy is realized in every litter.

MENDELIAN EXPECTATION CHART

been cleared from the pup's nostrils and mouth after the mother has licked her youngster clean; otherwise the pup may have difficulty breathing. If the mother fails to tear open the sac and stimulate the newborn's breathing, you can do this yourself by tearing the sack with your hands and then gently rubbing the infant with a soft, rough towel. The afterbirth attached to the puppy by the long umbilical cord, should follow the birth of each puppy. Watch to be sure that each afterbirth is expelled, for the retention of this material can cause infection. In her instinct for cleanliness the mother will probably eat the afterbirth after severing the umbilical cord. One or two meals of this will not hurt her; they stimulate her milk supply, as well as labor, for remaining pups. However, eating too many afterbirths can make her lose appetite for the food she needs to feed her pups and regain her strength. So remove the rest of

Prior to birth, the developing pups are housed in the horns of the uterus.

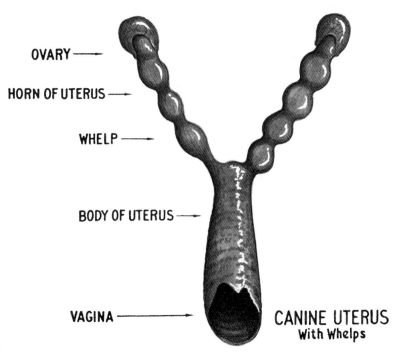

OVARY

HORN OF UTERUS

WHELP

BODY OF UTERUS

VAGINA

CANINE UTERUS
With Whelps

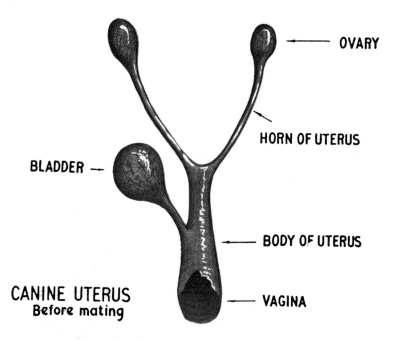

OVARY

HORN OF UTERUS

BLADDER —

BODY OF UTERUS

CANINE UTERUS
Before mating

VAGINA

The canine uterus is quite different from the human uterus. Besides the difference in shape, the canine uterus is designed to house an average of five to eight offspring.

them, along with the wet newspapers, and keep the box dry and clean.

If the mother does not bite the cord or bites it too close to the puppy's body, take over the job to prevent an umbilical hernia. Tearing is recommended, but you can cut the cord, about two inches from the body, with a sawing motion with scissors that have been sterilized in alcohol. Then dip the end of the cut cord in a shallow dish of iodine; the cord will dry up and fall off in a few days.

The puppies should follow each other at intervals of not more than half an hour. If more time goes past and you are sure there are still pups to come, taking the mother for a brisk walk outside may start labor again. If she is actively straining without producing a puppy, the youngster may be presented backward, a so-called "breech" birth. Careful assistance with a well-lubricated finger to feel for the puppy or to ease it back may help, but never attempt to pull it out by force. This could cause serious damage, so seek the services of an expert—your veterinarian or an experienced breeder.

Even the best planned breeding can bear unexpected problems and complications. Therefore, do not rely solely on textbook knowledge of breeding and genetics. Experienced breeders and veterinarians will generally lend their words of wisdom—take full advantage of their generosity. Mere trial and error is no basis for any responsible breeding program.

If *anything* seems wrong during labor or parturition, waste no time in calling your veterinarian, who will examine the bitch and, if necessary, give her hormones to stimulate the birth of the remaining puppies.

You may want his experience in whelping the litter even if all goes well. He will probably prefer to have the puppies born at his hospital rather than getting up in the middle of the night to come to your home. The mother would, no doubt, prefer to stay at home; but you can be sure she will get the best of care in a veterinary hospital. If the puppies are born at home, and all goes as it should, watch the mother carefully afterward. Within a day or two of the birth, it is wise to have the veterinarian check her and the pups to ensure that all is well.

Be sure each puppy finds a teat and starts nursing right away, as these first few meals supply colostral antibodies to help him fight disease. As soon

Cells reproduce by a process called mitosis, in which the cells divide, forming two identical cells.

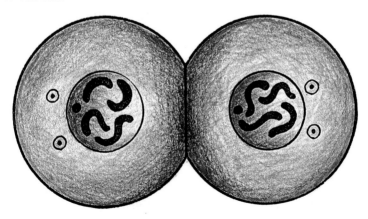

PUPPY GROWTH AND BREEDER RESPONSIBILITY	
AGE	**REQUIRED CARE/EXPECTED DEVELOPMENT**
WEEKS 1–2	Helpless; dam must provide constant care; owner must ensure warmth and cleanliness; puppy nurses, crawls, needs stimulation for elimination; sleeps 90% of time.
WEEKS 3–4	Owner sustains optimum environment; puppy is alert, laps from bowl, takes first steps; defecates on its own; baby teeth emerge; barks, wags tail.
WEEKS 4–5	Ambles, growls, and bites; play and interaction increase; human contact limited but essential; learning begins.
WEEKS 5–6	Weaning; human socialization vital; pack order apparent; sex play; explores and sleeps less.
WEEKS 6–8	Two to three daily meals; puppy accustomed to human family; breeder initiates housetraining; first veterinary visit; wary of the unknown.

as he is dry, hold each puppy to a nipple for a good meal without competition. Then he may join his littermates in the whelping box, out of his mother's way while she continues giving birth. Keep a supply of puppy formula on hand for emergency feedings or later weaning. An alternative formula of evaporated milk, corn syrup, and a little water with egg yolk can be warmed and fed if necessary. A pet nurser kit is also a good thing to have on hand; these are available at local pet shops. A supplementary feeding often helps weak pups (those that may have difficulty nursing) over the hump. Keep track of birth weights and weekly readings thereafter; this will furnish an accurate record of the pups' growth and health, and the information will be valuable to your veterinarian.

RAISING THE PUPPIES

After all the puppies have been born, take the mother outside for a walk and drink of water, and then return her to take care of her brood. She will probably not want to stay away for more than a minute or two for the first few weeks. Be sure to keep water available at all times and feed her milk or broth frequently, as she needs nourishment to produce milk. Encourage her to eat, with her favorite foods, until she seeks them of her own accord. She will soon develop a ravenous appetite and should have at least two large meals a day, with dry food available in addition. Your veterinarian can guide you on the finer points of nutrition as they apply to nursing dams.

Prepare a warm place to put the puppies after they are born to keep them dry and to help them to a good start in life. An electric heating pad, heat lamp or hot water bottle covered with flannel can be placed in the bottom of a cardboard box and near the mother so that she can see her puppies. She will usually allow you to help her care for the youngsters, but don't take them out of her sight. Let her handle things if your interference seems to make her nervous.

Be sure that all the puppies are getting enough to eat. If the mother sits or stands instead of lying still to nurse, the probable

While in the womb, each pup is encased in an individual protective sac.

cause is scratching from the puppies' nails. You can remedy this by clipping them, as you would the bitch's, with a pet nail clipper. Manicure scissors also do for these tiny claws. Some breeders advise disposing of the smaller or weaker pups in a large litter, as the mother has trouble handling more than six or seven. You can help her out by preparing an extra puppy box or basket furnished with a heating pad and/or heating lamp and some bedding material. Leave half the litter with the mother and the other half in the extra box, changing off at two-hour intervals at first. Later you may exchange them less frequently, leaving them all together except during the day. Try supplementary feedings, too. As soon as their eyes open, at about two weeks, they will lap from a small dish.

A puppy nurser kit is considered standard equipment by many breeders. These kits are available at your local pet shop.

WEANING THE PUPPIES

Normally the puppies should be completely weaned at five weeks, although you can start to feed them at three weeks. They will find it easier to lap semi-solid food than to drink milk at first, so mix baby cereal with whole or evaporated milk, warmed to body temperature, and offer it to the puppies in a saucer. Until they learn to lap it, it is best to feed one or two at a time because they are more likely to walk into it than to eat it. Hold the saucer at

their chin level, and let them gather around, keeping paws off the dish. Cleaning with a damp sponge afterward prevents most of the cereal from sticking to the pups if the mother doesn't clean them up. Once they have gotten the idea, broth or babies' meat soup may be alternated with milk, and you can start them on finely chopped meat. At about four weeks, they will eat four meals a day and soon do without their mother entirely. Start them on canned dog food, or leave dry puppy food with them in a dish for self-feeding. Don't leave the water dish with them all the time; at this age everything is a play toy and they will use it as a wading pool. They can drink all they need if it is offered several times a day, after meals. As the puppies grow up, the mother will go into their "pen" only to nurse them, first sitting up and then standing. To dry up her milk supply completely, keep the mother away for longer periods; after a few days of part-time nursing she can stay away for even longer periods, and then permanently. The little milk left will be resorbed by her body.

The puppies may be put outside during the day, unless it is too cold or rainy, as soon as their eyes are open. They will benefit from the sunlight. A rubber mat or newspapers underneath will protect them from cold or dampness. As they mature, the pups can be let out for longer intervals, although you must provide them with a shelter at night or in bad weather. By now, cleaning up after the matured youngsters is a man-sized job, so put them out at least during the day and make your task easier. If you enclose them in a run or kennel, remember to clean it *daily*, as various parasites and other infectious organisms may be lurking if the quarters are kept dirty.

You can expect the pups to need at least one worming before they are ready to go to new homes. Before the pups are three weeks old, take a stool sample from each to your veterinarian. The vet can determine, by analyzing the stool, if any of the pups have worms—and if so, what kind of worms are present. If one puppy is infected, then all should be wormed as a preventive measure. Follow the veterinarian's advice; this also applies to vaccinations. You will want to vaccinate the pups at the earliest possible age. This way, the pups destined for new homes will be protected against some of the more debilitating canine diseases.

THE DECISION TO SPAY OR NEUTER

If you decide not to use your male or female for breeding, or if you are obligated to have the animal altered based on an agreement made between you and the seller, make the necessary arrangements with your veterinarian as soon as possible. The surgery involved for both males and females is relatively simple and painless: males will be castrated and females will have their ovaries and uterus removed. In both

REASONS TO SPAY/NEUTER DOGS

- Reduces dog's need to roam.
- Reduces and/or eliminates certain reproductive cancers.
- Disburdens female dog of heat cycle and discomforts which accompany.
- Lessens dominance and mounting activity.
- Increases general lifespan of dog.
- Eliminates owner's concern of unwanted puppies, runaway stud dogs, stained furniture, nervous, and aggressive mood swings in pets.
- Relieves community of homeless dogs and property damage.

cases, the operation does not alter their personalities; you will, however, notice that males will be less likely to roam, to get into fights with other male dogs, and to mount objects and people.

Your veterinarian can best determine at what age neutering or spaying should be done. With a young female dog, the operation may be somewhat more involved, and as a result be more costly; however, in the long run you will be glad you made the decision to have this done for your pet. After a night or two at the veterinarian's or an animal hospital, your bitch can be safely returned to your home. Her stitches will heal in a short time, and when they are removed, you will hardly notice her souvenir scar of the routine operation. Once she has been spayed, she no longer will be capable of

having a litter of puppies.

Check with your city or town or with the local humane society for special programs that are available for pet owners. In many municipalities you can have your pet altered for just a small fee; the low price is meant to encourage pet owners to take advantage of this important means of birth control for their dogs. Pet adoption agencies and other animal welfare organizations can house only so many animals at one time, given the money, space, and other resources they have available. This is why pet owners are urged to have their pets altered, so that puppies resulting from accidental breedings won't end up being put to sleep as so many others have that are lost, stray, unwanted, or abandoned.

Traveling With Your Pet

Most pets can be trained to become very good travellers provided you begin that training when your pet is still very young. Unfortunately, your puppy's first ride in the car is likely to be to the veterinarian's where, after a frightening, abrupt introduction to the noisy, jolting automobile, he is stabbed by horrible long needles. Is there any wonder that, in the future, he will run for cover whenever he hears you jingling your car keys?

TRIPS BY CAR

Familiarize your pet with your car by taking him to a nearby park or an open area where he can run about and enjoy himself. Thus, you will have associated the car with something pleasant. Throw a dog biscuit or favorite toy into his crate, which you have placed on the back seat of the car, in an effort to preoccupy him. Never allow your dog to ride uncrated, as there is nothing more dangerous than a playful pup jumping on his owner as he is driving. Your puppy should also keep his head inside a moving car as dust and debris could irritate his eyes and nostrils.

When you park your car and leave your pet inside, make certain that the windows are open at least two inches; dogs are particularly susceptible to heat exhaustion and the

temperature in a parked car in the height of summer can reach over 120°F. Try to find a shady spot to park your car and return as soon as possible, as unscrupulous dognappers do exist who might pounce on your unsupervised pet. Of course, you must NEVER put your pet in the trunk of your car.

LONG TRIPS

When you prepare for a lengthy trip, make certain that you pack a few essential items for your canine companion: a blanket, a thermos of water, pet food, his food and water dishes, favorite toys, and any necessary medicine.

Do not give your pet a heavy meal before the trip but do ensure that he has a plentiful water supply. This will mean that you will have to break your journey several times so that he can relieve himself, but the rests and exercise will probably do you both good.

Most hotel chains in the United States welcome well-behaved pets but it is always wise to ask about their policy ahead of time when you make your reservation.

With early training and a little common sense, you and your pet will make excellent travelling companions *and* benefit from each other's company along the way.

BOARDING YOUR DOG

It may be necessary one day, however, to board your dog while you are on an extended vacation or business trip. In the United States, kennels which are members of the American Boarding Kennels Association should provide very good care for your pet. The A.B.K.A. is a nationwide non-profit organization established to promote high standards and professionalism in the pet-boarding industry.

Make certain to visit the kennels for an inspection before you board your dog. Examine the facilities, check the cleanliness of the stalls and exercise runs, talk to the owners about any special dietary or medical requirements your dog may have, look at the dogs staying there, and find out if there is a veterinarian on call. Also make your reservation well in advance, particularly if you plan to be away in the busy summer months or during the sometimes hectic holidays.

You can help your pet feel less homesick by taking his bed or favorite toy along. Finally, remember to leave an address or telephone number where you can be reached in case of an emergency.

Always include the dog's favorite toys in his crate whenever you travel by car.

Dog Books from t.f.h.

H-1016, 224 pp
135 photos

H-969, 224 pp
62 color photos

H-1061, 608 pp
Black/white photos

TS-101, 192 p
Over 100 pho

TW-102, 256 pp
Over 200 color

TW-113, 256 pp
200 color photos

H-962, 255 pp
Nearly 100 photos

SK-044, 64 pp
Over 50 color
photos

PS-872, 240 pp
178 color illustrations

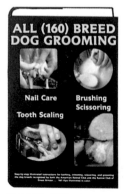

H-1095, 272 pp
Over 160 color illustrations

All-Breed Dog Books From T.F.H.

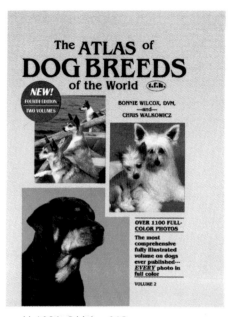

H-1091, 2 Vols., 912 pp
Over 1100 color photos

H-1106, 544 pp
Over 400 color photos

TS-175, 896 pp
Over 1300 color photos

The T.F.H. all-breed dog books are the most comprehensive and colorful of all dogs books available. The most famous of these recent publications, *The Atlas of Dog Breeds of the World,* written by Dr. Bonnie Wilcox and Chris Walkowicz, is now available as a two-volume set. Now in its fourth edition, the *Atlas* remains one of the most sought-after gift books and reference works in the dog world.

A very successful spinoff of the *Atlas* is *The Mini-Atlas of Dog Breeds,* written by Andrew De Prisco and James B. Johnson. This compact but comprehensive book has been praised and recommended by most national dog publications for its utility and reader-friendliness. The true field guide for dog lovers.

Canine Lexicon by the authors of the *Mini-Atlas* is an up-to-date encyclopedic dictionary for the dog person. It is the most complete single volume on the dog ever published covering more breeds than any other book as well as other relevant topics, including health, showing, training, breeding, anatomy, veterinary terms, and much more. No dog book before has ever offered this many stunning color photographs of all breeds, dog sports, and topics (over 1300 in full color).

Index